84

Lewis Carroll

POSTHUMOUS PORTRAIT, 1899, BY SIR HUBERT HERKOMER
AT CHRIST CHURCH, OXFORD

The Story of
LEWIS CARROLL

by

ROGER LANCELYN GREEN

Author of
Tellers of Tales, Andrew Lang

HENRY SCHUMAN
New York

*Published in the United States
of America by*

HENRY SCHUMAN

1951

To

My own Oxford Child-Friends

Past and Present

:

TONI

DIANA

JANET

ANNE

ANNA

JOANNA

BARBARA

SUSAN

ISABEL

KARIN

NEIL

JACKIE

PEGGIE LOU

—

Merton College

OXFORD

1947

CONTENTS

CHAPTER I

THE CHESHIRE CHILD

IF you happen to visit the little Cheshire village of Daresbury
—now, alas, on the very outskirts of smoky, industrial
Warrington—and have the curiosity to explore the parish
church, you will come upon surely the most unexpected
stained-glass window that any church can boast. For under
the main window, which shows the first Christmas scene in
the stable at Bethlehem, are five small panels of stained
glass : the first contains accurate and authentic portraits
of the White Rabbit and the Dodo, with little Bill the
Lizard shooting out of the chimney between them ; and
next in order are the Caterpillar and the Fish Footman ; in
the centre panel is the Mad Hatter (wearing only one shoe,
and carrying a tea-cup) with the March Hare opposite,
and between them the Dormouse dozing peacefully in the
tea-pot ; then come the Duchess and the Mock Turtle,
with the Gryphon spreading his wings between them ; and,
last of all, the supercilious Knave of Hearts smiling at the
Queen (who is obviously shouting " Off with his head ! "),
while separating them is the grinning Cheshire Cat, still
triumphant over all executioners—for only his head is
visible !

But if you look closely, you will discover the reason
for this odd example of church decoration. For just above
Bill the Lizard's nose is an inscription : " In memory of
Charles Lutwidge Dodgson (Lewis Carroll), Author of
Alice in Wonderland " ; and over the Cheshire Cat's head
the words : " He was born at Daresbury Parsonage,

1

Jan. 27, 1832, and died at Guildford, Jan. 14, 1898." On the left hand side of the main window you will recognise Charles Dodgson himself, with Alice beside him, kneeling in prayer at the stable in Bethlehem ; while, to add another touch of solemnity, each of the three centre panels contains, in place of the inscriptions, an open book bearing a verse from Lewis Carroll's serious poem " Christmas Greetings from a Fairy to a Child." The Mad Hatter and the March Hare, for example, carry this verse :—

> " We have heard the children say—
> Gentle children whom we love—
> Long ago, on Christmas Day,
> Came a message from above."

Daresbury church is no longer the same in which Charles Dodgson's father preached, for a new one was built in 1851, and of the square, homely looking parsonage only the gate posts remain ; but the village itself has not quite lost its old remoteness, its atmosphere of being in the very heart of the country, even though the growing town has nearly reached it.

When Charles was a little boy, however, Warrington was a good seven miles away, and even the parsonage stood in the middle of fields, a mile and a half from the village :

> " An island farm, 'mid seas of corn,
> Swayed by the wandering breath of morn,
> The happy spot where I was born."

as he pictured it many years later in the red glow of his fire.

How lonely and self-contained life was in such a spot a hundred years ago is very hard to imagine now. Charles was the eldest of a family of eleven—with seven sisters and three brothers—and so had far more companionship than some children of the period ; but outside his family, the only regular visitors seem to have been the Reverend Thomas Bayne, Headmaster of Warrington Grammar School, who was in the habit of coming to

2

Daresbury to assist with the services, and his little boy, Vere, about three years older than Charles, who became his life-long friend.

But otherwise, the family, living in the quiet parsonage in the midst of the pleasant, well-wooded meadows of Cheshire, formed almost its own world, and looked to itself for its own amusements as for its own comfort and its own approach to life. For the family in those days was a much closer and more important unity than it has become now,—and throughout his life Charles was a dutiful and thoughtful member of his family.

There was his father, the Rev. Charles Dodgson, later an archdeacon, a kindly, humorous man, but strict to the

MRS. DODGSON
From a silhouette

smallest detail—loving his children none the less for the rule of iron which he exercised over them, and the respect with which he would consider it natural for them to treat him. And Charles was truly fond of his father, regarding him with affection as well as with the respect which he considered his natural duty.

Mrs. Dodgson was a less noticeable figure, and hardly anything about her has been preserved : but just as strong a bond of sympathy existed between her and Charles. She was " one of the sweetest and gentlest women that ever lived, whom to know was to love. . . . It has been said by

3

her children that they never in all their lives remember to have heard an impatient or harsh word from her lips." And one sees how Charles felt about her from the fact that for years one of his most treasured possessions was a letter which she had written to him as a small boy, while she was on a visit to her father-in-law. On the outside of the letter Charles wrote : " No one is to touch this note, for it belongs to C.L.D.", and then, feeling that even this might not be enough to prevent his little sisters from meddling with it, he added : " Covered with slimy pitch so that they will wet their fingers "—a method of preserving letters truly novel, and all his own invention !

In his earliest years Charles must have been a very solitary child—certainly until his sisters were old enough to be companionable—for his eldest brother was at least five years younger than himself. And so, to begin with, Charles amused himself in a variety of odd ways, making intimate friends with such unlikely creatures as snails and toads ; while in his anxiety to assist a number of earthworms who seemed anxious to make war on one another in a big way, he supplied them each with a little piece of pipe as a weapon ! Such quaint friendships invented by lonely children are not at all unusual, and one is reminded of another famous writer, Mrs. Molesworth, who, when a little girl, considered that her dearest friends were the reels of cotton in her mother's workbox !

Living in a very pious family, and being the son of a parson, Charles must from his earliest days have heard much talk of assistance to the poor of the parish ; for at that time there was far greater distress and poverty than there is now, and those who were better off spent much time in charitable attempts to assist those who deserved their help. Charles was also determined to join in the good work, and he proceeded to peel a large number of rushes, explaining that the pith could now " be given to the poor," though

4

he never informed anyone what use " the poor " were expected to make of it !

At the earliest possible age Charles's education was begun by his mother and father : reading and writing to begin with, followed by " the different branches of arithmetic "— just as in the case of the Mock Turtle, though for Charles these would hardly have been " Ambition, Distraction, Uglification and Derision " !

From the beginning Mathematics was Charles's favourite subject : once, when he was a very small boy indeed, he found a book of logarithms and brought it to his father to be explained ; Mr. Dodgson told him that he was much too young to understand anything about such a difficult subject. The child listened to what his father said, and still insisted, " *But*, please explain ! "

One must not think, however, that Charles was anything but a natural child ; Victorian children were very much more sedate than we are now, and very much more serious too. A great number of their lessons were abominably dull, but they do seem to have taken a far greater pleasure and pride in learning than their descendants. Partly, this was due to the fact that in those days they had so few other possible things which they were allowed to do ; there were very few story books, and most of these taught a very definite lesson of one kind or another ; and, of course, they were given far less freedom and expected to behave with infinitely more decorum.

CHARLES, AGED 8
From a silhouette

But in spite of the many restrictions, Charles managed to

spend much of his time climbing trees and messing about in the clay and water of the old marl-pits which are to be found in nearly every field in Cheshire. And once, before Charles was eleven, the whole family went away for a holiday to Beaumaris in the island of Anglesey, which must have been a very great event in their quiet lives. The journey took three days, for there were no railways for them to use, and they still had to travel in a stage coach ; one can imagine Charles's excitement, particularly when crossing the great new suspension bridge over the Menai Straits—and perhaps one of the innumerable questions he would have been asking was how all those great chains and bars were kept from getting rusty—though it was probably still some years before he had

> " completed his design
> To keep the Menai bridge from rust
> By boiling it in wine " !

And how exciting he must have found Beaumaris itself, with its wonderful old castle all covered in ivy, with long dark passages built in the thickness of the walls running all round it, with a hundred and one ups and downs and un-accountable corners—to say nothing of the dungeons going deep down into the darkness, rather more like the entrance to Wonderland than any gently sloping rabbit-hole !

Life at Daresbury must have seemed even quieter and more uneventful after such a holiday, though that itself was about to change. For when Charles was eleven Mr. Dodgson was made rector of Croft in Durham on the river Tees, just over the border from Yorkshire—a much bigger place than Daresbury, and far less lonely and secluded ; and a little later he was made Archdeacon of Richmond and a Canon of Ripon Cathedral.

So the family moved into the Rectory of Croft, a large brick building with a red tiled roof set in the middle of a most beautiful garden full of fruit trees and rare flowers, and this was Charles's home until he was a grown man and settled at Oxford— though, of course, the time for going to boarding school was near at hand.

But his main interests, outside his actual work, were always centered round the family at Croft, even during his earlier years at Oxford, and he had at least one year there of freedom before being sent away to school at the age of twelve. And by this time the in-

Fair stands the ancient Rectory,
The Rectory of Croft.

creasing family was growing old enough to require entertainment, and, even at so early an age Charles didn't find any difficulty in amusing children younger than himself and entering into their games with that complete seriousness without which the elder can never be accepted as an equal.

Chief and earliest among the games at Croft was the railway in the garden. Trains in 1843 were still a new and exciting invention, and Charles was never far behind the times: so he constructed a train out of a wheel-barrow, a barrel and a small truck, and conveyed his small passengers from station to station round about the garden; insisting that they must buy tickets before getting into the train, and allowing them time to visit the refreshment room at each station. And being even then oddly careful, as he showed himself later with all his lists and registers, he also prepared a book of "Railway Rules," one at least of which (Number 3) has been preserved: "Station master must mind his station and supply refreshments: he can put anyone who behaves badly to prison, while a train goes round the garden: he

7

must ring for the passengers to take their seats, then count 20 slowly, then ring again for the train to start. The 'L' one shall be a surgeon, the wounded must be brought there gratis by the next train going that way and cured gratis. There shall be a place at the 'L' station for lost luggage. If there is anyone to go, a flag is to be hoisted." We cannot guess now what "the 'L' one" means, but the other parts of Rule 3 are delightfully precise—and there obviously would be any number of "wounded" lying about in the quiet garden of Croft !

Another of Charles's amusements was conjuring, and he used to entertain the family, and occasionally friends, with many clever tricks, for which "sleight-of-hand" his long white fingers were ideally suited. As a conjuror Charles would dress up in a brown wig and a long white robe ; for his interest in acting seems to have been born with him and was not discouraged, even though Mr. Dodgson disapproved of theatres, and never allowed any of his children to visit one while they were under his control.

Even amateur theatricals, if tolerated, were not encouraged ; but puppet shows did not come under the same disapproval, and Charles delighted in puppets. He was a clever carpenter, even at the age of ten, and (with a little help from a professional joiner) he made a wooden marionette theatre $26\frac{1}{2}$ inches wide, 23 inches high and 18 inches deep. Although the theatre was home-made, Charles did not disdain the improvements which "Toy Theatre" sheets, printed in bright colours on thin cardboard, would make. These could be bought easily and cheaply (including pages of figures at "a penny plain or twopence colored"), and he used a set (probably printed in Germany) for his proscenium, for three pairs of "wings" and one "backdrop," pasting them all on to thin wood, with an alternative scene stuck on the other side of the "wings" and "backdrop." For "footlights" in the front of the stage he fixed little tin shades to hold candle-ends, and there were eleven cardboard characters moved by wires from above. The "twopence colored" Toy-Theatre figures he merely cut out and steered with the wires; but he also made a few wooden puppets, working the whole show himself, his clever white fingers moving deftly among the numerous strings and wires.

He wrote his own plays, too, the most popular one being *The Tragedy of King John*, which was probably adapted from Shakespeare, but seems now to have been lost. Another play, however, which is still in existence, was entirely his own invention: a comic "Ballad Opera" called *La Guida di Bragia* or, translating out of his "original" Italian, "Bradshaw's Railway Guide." This is a very slight and humble affair, though clever enough for a boy of ten, and consists of an amusing series of parodies of well-known poems, the whole play centring delightfully about railways and railway stations. The plot is concerned with Mooney and Spooney, who are banished from court and become railway porters, their particular job being to sing all day so as to entertain the travellers. At their railway station, however, everything is in a continual muddle; the travellers include Orlando and his wife Sophonisba, the latter dreadfully concerned over an Irish stew which she has told her maid to prepare for their return; there is also a Kaffir who talks a language that neither Mooney nor Spooney can understand; and "Mrs. Muddle," a fussy old lady who always uses the wrong words, demanding that before she enters the train she must have her life "ensnared." Mooney and Spooney are so concerned that they forget to sing—and immediately all the trains begin to run at the wrong times, and the luggage is always lost. Orlando tries to assert himself, singing:

> "Should all my luggage be forgot,
> And never come to hand,

9

I'll never quit this fatal spot,
                But perish where I stand ! "
But the confusion grows and grows until finally La
Guida di Bragia comes to life and takes control of the
station, explaining to the horror-stricken Mooney and
Spooney, and all the travellers :—

        " I made a rule my servants were to sing :
        That rule they disobeyed, and in revenge
        I altered all the train times in my book ! "

Besides writing plays for his marionette theatre, Charles
began at about the same time to edit a series of family
magazines of which he seems to have written nearly all the
contents himself. The earliest was called *Useful and
Instructive Poetry*, and was begun just before he went to his
first school in 1845 ; and it was followed by a whole procession of others of which only the names survive. All were
written by hand—apparently by Charles's hand—and
usually consisted of loose sheets roughly bound up, though
in later years ready-made volumes were used. Even when
Charles was at Oxford he continued to make " magazines "
for the younger members of the family, though by then the
volumes were much more in the nature of scrap-books into
which he copied or pasted poems and stories already
published. Of these Oxford ventures the last two still
survive—*The Rectory Umbrella*, started " in 1849 or 1850,"
and *Misch-Masch*, begun in 1855.

These two magazines, particularly the first, are fully
illustrated by Charles with amusing and forceful drawings,
and it is probable that earlier lost ones also contained
pictures. All his life he took a great interest in drawing,
though his own efforts were never good enough to publish,
and this must have been another of his earliest amusements.
The Mock-Turtle learnt " Drawling, Stretching, and Faint-
ing in Coils " quite as a matter of course, and although art
was more of a " lady-like " accomplishment, it was taught

much more generally than it is now, and Charles's sisters would certainly have learnt Drawing and Sketching—even if, for them, Painting in Oils ranked as " an extra."

And so the first twelve years of Charles Dodgson's life passed happily enough, at first in the quiet wonderland of a little country parish, and then in the scarcely less quiet rectory with the big garden at Croft.

He seems to have been a quiet, thoughtful, rather serious little boy, and in some ways a trifle old for his age. There is no record that he ever got into trouble at home, and he had very few playmates except his sisters (for his next brother was six years younger than he), but nevertheless he was very much of a proper country boy, for he lived a vigorous life, climbing trees, falling into the pond, carpentering, and taking part in many other delightful occupations which a farm has to offer. He was also interested in new things—and trains in the Eighteen-forties were every bit as new and exciting to a boy of ten as jet-propelled 'planes are to us a hundred years later.

But Charles Dodgson had also a vivid imagination, which led him often into a dream world of his own contriving, though, a rare thing among small boys, he was willing to admit other children into it; and he was already a keen scholar, particularly in mathematics which was afterwards to become his life's work at Oxford. And above all, he was starting, even at the early age of ten, to become an expert at writing stories and plays and humorous poems to amuse small children : all these things the unconscious beginning of the real Lewis Carroll.

CHAPTER II

THE SCHOOL-BOY EDITOR

AT twelve it was time for Charles Dodgson to go to a preparatory school, and Richmond was chosen as being not far from Croft and very well known in its day.

It was a pleasant school, particularly as schools went a century ago, and Charles seems to have been very happy during his two years there. Richmond is still a charming old country town with cobbled streets and a tall ruined castle— not too much of a change for the country boy coming to live in a town for the first time.

Nor was the school itself too wildly different from home life in the rectory full of children; Mr. Tate, the headmaster, had seven children including one girl, all of whom mixed freely in the school, where the boys ranged in ages from seven to fourteen. Of course, as a " new boy," Charles had many small discomforts and trials to undergo, such as those of which he wrote to two of his sisters in one of his first letters home (August 5, 1844).

" . . . The boys have played two tricks upon me which were these—they first proposed to play at ' King of the Cobblers ' and asked if I would be king, to which I agreed. Then they made me sit down and sat (on the ground) in a circle round me, and told me to say ' Go to work ' which I said, and they immediately began kicking me and knocking me on all sides. The next game they proposed was ' Peter, the red lion,' and they made a mark on a tombstone (for we were playing in the churchyard) and one of the boys walked with his eyes shut, holding out his finger, trying to touch the mark ; at last it was my turn ; they told me to shut my eyes well, and the next minute I had my finger in the mouth

12

of one of the boys, who had stood (I believe) before the tombstone with his mouth open."

Charles did not say that the boy bit him, but that is probably what he meant; bullying was much more general at schools then than it is now, but Richmond seems to have been fairly free and Charles had as yet little experience of it, though he does list the " chief games " as being " football, wrestling, leap-frog and fighting."

With the school work he found little difficulty either then or later, though writing and construing Latin verse (which has only recently ceased to be the chief basis of Classical education in schools) did not come very easily to him, and he is said to have preferred his own methods of scanning to the accepted ones of Virgil and Ovid! However, Mr. Tate, the headmaster, wrote enthusiastically to Charles's father, expressing the opinion that Charles possessed " a very uncommon share of genius " ; and described him as " gentle and cheerful in his intercourse with others, playful and ready in conversation, he is capable of acquirements and knowledge far beyond his years, while his reason is so clear and so jealous of error, that he will not rest satisfied without a most exact solution of whatever appears to him obscure."

While he was still at Richmond Charles saw his first work in print, a story of " a sensational type " called *The Unknown One*, published in the School Magazine in 1845, but alas no copy of it has survived.

Charles was at Richmond for two years, and he spoke of them afterwards as being happy years and of Mr. Tate as his " kind old schoolmaster." But his experiences at Rugby, which followed, were, unfortunately, of a very different kind, and he wrote a few years later : " I cannot say that I look back on my life at a Public School with any sensations of pleasure, or that any earthly considerations would induce me to go through my three years again."

Charles kept no diary during these years, and very little

13

has been discovered or preserved about his experiences at Rugby, but we can get a good and reasonably accurate picture from *Tom Brown's Schooldays* in which the events described happened only about ten years earlier.

We can picture Charles arriving by stage-coach after a day or more spent in travelling, and being greeted as he entered the gate with the stock questions reserved for all new boys : " You fellow, what's your name ? Where do you come from ? How old are you ? Where do you board and what form are you in ? " Then, if he were lucky enough to know any of the older boys who could put him up to the usual routine, he would go out and buy the regulation top hats, two being allowed each "half," at a cost of seven-and-six each.

Being a new boy, Charles became a " fag " immediately, and was expected to run errands for one of the bigger boys, clean out the study, and even perhaps do some of the Latin impositions for his lord and master—who would throw boots at his head if he neglected any of these duties. Charles himself had a study before long which he shared with one or two other boys of his own age : small and rather uncomfortable little rooms they were, and miserably cold, as the only heat came from a single fire at the end of the corridor—which the prefect (called at Rugby a " prælector ") was in the habit of monopolising by means of a curtain stretched across to divert all the warmth in through his open door.

As for the study itself, " it wasn't very large certainly, being about six feet long by four broad. It couldn't be called light, as there were bars and a grating to the window. . . . The space under the window at the farther end was occupied by a square table with a reasonably clean and whole red-and-blue check table cloth ; a hard-seated sofa covered with red stuff occupied one side, running up to the end, and making a seat for one, or by sitting close for two, at the table ; and a good stout wooden chair afforded a seat to another boy, so that three could sit and work together. The walls were wainscoted half-way up, the wainscot being covered with green baize, the remainder with a bright-patterned paper . . . Over the door were a row of hat-pegs, and on each side bookcases with cupboards at the bottom."

Dinner was in the middle of the day, and at a quarter-past one the bell began to toll for the boys to assemble in the hall, where Charles, as a new boy, found his place next to the præpositor at the end of one of the tables, and sat taking his first view of his future school fellows in a body. " In they came, some hot and ruddy from football or long walks, some pale and chilly from hard reading in their studies," a master at the table called the names, and then sat reading a book all the time he was eating ; and when he got up and walked over to the fire, Charles could give his full attention to the other small boys round him, " some of whom were reading, and the rest talking in whispers to one another, or stealing one another's bread, or shooting pellets, or digging their forks through the tablecloth."

In the afternoon came football, a very violent and barbarous game in those days, with few rules except for the methods of scoring goals, and often with as many as a hundred and twenty boys on one side against a team of fifty or sixty. Moreover, as one of the older boys informed Tom Brown, " it's no joke playing-up in a match, I can tell you. Quite another thing from your private school games. Why, there's been two collar-bones broken this half, and a dozen fellows lamed. And last year a fellow had his leg broken." Even when not playing football Charles was com-pelled to watch every game, which must have wasted a great deal of his time. He was no use himself as a footballer, while at cricket it is recorded that he only played once, when he was put on to bowl but taken off after one ball, the captain remarking that " the ball, if it had gone far enough, would have been a wide !"

But the most unpleasant side of public school life a hundred years ago was the bullying and the callousness which the older boys practised on the younger ones, of which many examples may be found in *Tom Brown's Schooldays*. Some at least of these must have come Charles Dodgson's way ; but as he grew older the effect which any such early sufferings had on him was to make him a zealous champion and defender of the younger boys ; and when he left Rugby early in 1849 he left behind him the reputation of being well able to use his fists in a just cause.

The sufferings of his first few terms—the one which he recalled particularly being the practice of the elder boys of removing the blankets from the beds of the juniors to keep themselves warm in winter—and other petty annoyances which made the nights as hard to endure as the days, did not prevent him from working hard and with good results. In spite of the rather dull and unimaginative routine and traditions then very much in force at the Public Schools, and the absurd waste of time involved in the compulsory writing out of hundreds of Latin lines as impositions for the most trifling offences, or even for mistakes in form work, Charles managed to achieve an excellent standard of learning. He said afterwards that he never worked at Rugby with any enjoyment, but for all that he seldom returned home at the end of any term without bringing at least one prize with him.

Some of his life at Rugby he enjoyed, however ; he wrote home on at least one occasion of a pleasant evening spent with Mr. Smythies, the second mathematical master, who entertained him and another boy with wine, figs and kindly conversation ; and on another of the books which he happened to be reading at the moment, in the little spare time that the school authorities allowed, which were

16

David Copperfield in its original monthly parts and the latest volume of Macaulay's *History of England*.

But he felt mainly relief when he left Rugby in 1849 to spend nearly two years at home before proceeding to Oxford, though the Headmaster, Dr. Tait, had made special note of his career at the school, and wrote to Charles's father : " I must not allow your son to leave school without expressing to you the very high opinion I entertain of him . . . both of his abilities and upright conduct. His mathematical knowledge is great for his age, and I doubt not he will do himself credit in classics. As I believe I mentioned to you before, his examination for the Divinity prize was one of the most creditable exhibitions I have ever seen. During the whole time of his being at my house his conduct has been excellent."

Charles spent most of the next two years living quietly at Croft and preparing for his career at Oxford, but he did find time to produce another household magazine for his ten brothers and sisters. This, *The Rectory Umbrella*, was easily the most ambitious so far, though nothing contained in it seemed to him worth publishing later or using again in after years ; some of the verses, however, are included in various modern editions of " Lewis Carroll's " works, the best of them being his very amusing parody of Macaulay's poem *Horatius*.

In one set of verses, which is not included in any of the collected editions, he explained how the new magazine differed from the earlier ones. of his school-days, and described some of those which went before :

" First in age, but not in merit,
　　　Stands the Rect'ry Magazine ;
　All its wit thou dost inherit
　　　Though the Comet came between. . .

17

Next in order comes the Comet,
    Like some vague and feverish dream,
Gladly, gladly turn I from it,
    To behold thy rising beam !
When I first began to edit,
    In the Rect'ry Magazine,
Each one wrote therein who read it
    Each one read who wrote therein.

When the Comet next I started,
    They grew lazy as a drone ;
Gradually all departed,
    Leaving me to write alone.
But in thee—let future ages
    Mark the fact which I record,
No one helped me in thy pages,
    Even with a single word ! "

There is nothing very unusual in a family of children
writing their own magazine, and long before the Lewis
Carroll magazines became famous both Dickens in *Holiday
Romance* and E. Nesbit in *The Treasure Seekers* had invented
examples which in many ways are really rather like *The
Rectory Umbrella*—with a serial thriller (Charles called his
"The Walking-stick of Destiny," but he combined his ready
gift of humor with the lurid tale of a wicked Baron), and
serious poems that are really comic (but again, Charles's
are intentionally funny), and the series of "Informative
Articles"—in which yet again the irresistible humor breaks
through.

But indeed there is a little spark of the real Lewis Carroll
humor in nearly all of it, though of course it is not yet well
developed and is often crude and badly handled. Yet the
"Horatius" poem proves that he had already some skill
in handling parody—which afterwards came to such per-

18

A DRAWING FROM THE RECTORY UMBRELLA

fection in " Father William " and " The Aged, Aged Man " —and at least of interest is the fact that one of the "serious" articles deals with a bird well known to us from *Alice*— the Lory :

" This creature is, we believe, a species of parrot," wrote Charles. " The time and place of the Lory's birth is uncertain ; the egg from which it was hatched was most probably, to judge from the colour of the bird, one of those magnificent Easter eggs which our readers have doubtless often seen ; the experiment of hatching an Easter egg is at any rate worth trying." Next he gave an amusing account of the Lory in a long poem by Robert Southey (who also wrote the original of " Father William "), described a stuffed specimen which most of his readers had seen in the museum at York, and then ended : " Having thus stated all we know, and a good deal we don't know, on this interesting subject, we must conclude : our next subject will probably be Fishes."

The humorous poems, which are the best things in *The Rectory Umbrella*, were in most cases topical—that is, concerned with the doings of the family at Croft. One series of poems was begun under the general title of " Lays of Sorrow," and the first of these told of how " two stalwart youths "—a couple of the younger Dodgson boys— constructed a new hen-house, and how, to everyone's consternation, one of the chickens was found dead—which gave rise to a " trial scene " in the midst of which one of Charles's sisters burst into the room where the rest of the family was debating of suicide or murder, with the news

> " That nasty hen has been and gone
> And killed another chicken ! "

And this was preceded by a delightful touch, very typical of Charles, when having said that the old tree is split into perches " At a hundred strokes a minute," he adds a footnote: "At the rate of a stroke and two-thirds in a second." And when the first chicken is found dead, its master's sorrow is compared with that of—

> ". . . one, whose ticket's marked ' Return,'
> When to the lonely roadside station
> He flies in fear and perturbation,
> Thinks of his home—the hissing urn—
> Then runs with flying hat and hair,
> And entering, finds to his despair
> He's missed the very latest train ! "

Indeed, Charles Dodgson's interest in trains continues through all his books, right up to *Sylvie and Bruno*, and there are very few which do not contain some reference to loco-motives, when even the life of the Snark is threatened with " a railway share ! "

But the best thing in *The Rectory Umbrella* was the Parody of " Horatius " which appeared as " Lays of Sorrow : No. 2." This was also based on an incident in the life at Croft—the attempt of one of Charles's brothers to ride a particularly stubborn donkey. The rider was probably Skeffington, the eldest brother (who was a baby when Charles, from Richmond school, wrote him the short and forceful letter : " Roar not, lest thou be abolished ")— for when the donkey proved unmanageable, the next brother, Wilfred Langley, came to his aid, together with a sister [Louisa ?] ; as the poem has it :

> " Then out spake Ulfrid Longbow,
>   A valiant youth was he,
> ' Lo ! I will stand on thy right hand,
>   And guard the pass for thee.'
> And out spake fair Flureeza,
>   His sister eke was she,
> ' I will abide on thy other side,
>   And turn thy steed for thee.' "

Exeter College; and the second of these wrote of Oxford as he first remembered it: "On all sides, except where it touched the railway, the city ended abruptly, as if a wall had been about it, and you came suddenly upon the meadows. There was little brick in the city, it was either grey with stone or yellow with the wash of pebble-dash in the poorer streets. It was an endless delight to us to wander about the streets, where there were still many old houses with wood carving and a little sculpture here and there . . . The buildings of Merton and the Cloisters of New College were our chief shrines in Oxford . . . "

University life in those days was very different also: "The position of the undergraduates was much more similar to that of schoolboys than is now the case," wrote Charles's nephew in 1898; "they were subject to the same penalties— corporal punishment, even, had only just gone out of vogue ! —and were expected to work, and to work hard."

Of course, many undergraduates did not work hard— particularly the rich ones, who spent most days of the week in fox-hunting, ratting with terriers, and other such amusements, and most evenings in gambling, playing billiards and holding hilarious drinking parties in one another's rooms. This wild form of life is very well described in one of the best known stories of Victorian Oxford, *Mr. Verdant Green* by "Cuthbert Bede," and although Charles was always one of the most hard-working and retiring of undergraduates, many of the same experiences befell him as befell Verdant while becoming acquainted with college customs and University procedure.

Probably, as he came from the north, Charles travelled to Oxford by stage-coach (the Birmingham railway was not opened until his second year), and on arriving he went out immediately to buy a "cap and gown," without which no undergraduate even today may dine in the college hall, enter the college chapel, or attend lectures and tutorials.

THE DINING HALL AT CHRIST CHURCH, OXFORD

The next step was to find which rooms had been allotted to him—a very small bed-room and a rather larger sitting-room from which, in all probability, the bed-room had been divided at some time since the college was built; interview his "scout," as the college servants are called; superintend the unpacking of his luggage and boxes of books; and then go down for his first dinner in the great panelled hall which had been built in the reign of Henry VIII.

"In those days," wrote Charles's nephew, "the under-graduates dining in hall were divided into 'messes.' Each mess consisted of about half a dozen men, who had a table to themselves. Dinner was served at five, and very indifferently served too; the dishes and plates were of pewter, and the joint was passed round, each man cutting off what happened he wanted for himself. In Mr. Dodgson's mess were Philip Pusey, the late Rev. G. C. Woodhouse, and, among others, one who still lives in *Alice in Wonderland* as the Hatter. . . ."

All the food was not handed round, and on his first night in hall perhaps Charles, like Verdant Green, was so much "wrapped up in the novelty of the scene, that he ran a great risk of losing his dinner. The scouts fled about in all directions with plates, and glasses, and pewter dishes, and massive silver mugs that had gone round the tables for the last two centuries, and still no one waited upon Mr. Verdant Green. He twice timidly ventured to say, 'Waiter!' but no one answered to his call, and as he was too bashful and occupied with his own thoughts to make another attempt, it is probable that he would have risen from dinner as unsatis-fied as when he sat down, had not his right-hand companion (having partly relieved his own wants) perceived his neigh-bour to be a freshman, and kindly said to him, 'I think you'd better begin your dinner, because we don't stay here long. What is your scout's name?' And when he had been told it, he turned to Filcher and asked him 'What the

deuce do you mean by not waiting on your
which, with the addition of a few gratuitous threa
effect of bringing the scout to perform his duties.'

During the long evening which followed Charles would
return to his rooms and work until midnight, or even later,
leaving the wilder parties wisely alone, but going
occasionally to drink a glass of wine with a few friends and
discuss the studies on which they were engaged, or questions
of Theology and literature.

On the first night, however, when Charles was still learning the ways of Oxford, some well meaning undergraduate
probably gave him the same advice as Mr. Verdant Green
received in preparation for the next morning : " When they
ring you up sharp for chapel don't you lose any time about
your washing . . . just jump into a pair of bags and Welling-
tons ; clap a top coat on you, and button up to the chin,
and there you are, ready dressed in the twinkling of a bed-
post ! " For in those days attendance at morning chapel was
compulsory—though Charles did not find this an unpleasant
duty, and only mentions one occasion on which he overslept
and failed to put in an appearance—thus laying himself
open to a reprimand or even an imposition.

As the undergraduates filed into the chapel (the little
Norman cathedral at Christ Church, which stood there long
before the college was built round it), they noticed that
" on either side of the door were two men, who quickly
glanced at each one who passed, and as quickly pricked a
mark against his name on the chapel lists. As the freshman
went by, they made a careful study of his person." Only a
few years later Charles, as one of the junior Students of
Christ Church, had himself to " prick bills " for the undergraduates attending chapel—and found himself even then
liable to an imposition if he or any of the eight most recently
elected Students neglected this duty.

Nowadays one is not made to attend chapel : instead, on

thirty mornings in the term (and there are forty-eight altogether, excluding Sundays) you must be up and dressed in time to appear, wearing a gown (and a tie and trousers —even if you have still got pyjamas underneath !) between 7.55 and 8 a.m. to sign your name on a list in a college lecture room still in the presence of one of the junior Students (or "Fellows" as they are called at every college except Christ Church). During those five minutes a bell rings—and you are too late if the last stroke of the college clock has sounded before you enter the room. Experience proves that you can jump out of bed when the bell begins to ring, and enter the lecture-room fully dressed while the clock is still striking . . . Many undergraduates return to bed after "call-over," and slumber undisturbed for another hour or more— having previously left orders with their scout to leave a cold breakfast in the next room.

Charles Dodgson, however, did not return to bed ; indeed, he was in the habit of being called at a quarter past six, of being ready for the day by seven, and of having breakfast before attending chapel. Even while he was an undergraduate he usually worked at least until midnight ; and in later years he needed less and less sleep, often working until three in the morning, and still rising without any difficulty between six and seven. Besides the work which they were expected to do in their own rooms and during the vacations, undergraduates were required to attend a large number of compulsory lectures and to be present from time to time in the "Examination Schools" where third or fourth year men were being examined orally for their degrees— a practice which has long ceased to be performed in public, just as the undergraduate of today can in most cases, ignore, if he wishes, the fact that a single lecturer exists in the University. But the work expected in those days was far narrower and more specialised than now : so narrow and dry and unimaginative in many cases that only young men like Charles Dodgson could study it with any enthusiasm, or feel that Oxford was doing them much good. To William Morris and Edward Burne-Jones at Exeter College, for example, as to others of their friends such as R. W. Dixon and Cormell Price, Oxford seemed a dead, cramping place, hundreds of years behind the times, an enemy to the new and wonderful ideas about art and life which meant so much to them.

Charles did not know these other undergraduates and their group of friends, and although he met and liked some of them in later years, he would never have been one of them in the early days. Oxford as he found it suited him well enough in most ways—and he suited Oxford well enough never to feel out of harmony with it, though he was always ready to criticise anything about the University which he considered should be altered or improved for the general well-being of the whole.

All the work expected of him as an undergraduate was not quite to his taste ; for besides Mathematics and Theology, his chosen subjects, he was expected to pass examinations in Greek and Latin Literature, ancient history and philosophy. In Mathematics he took First Class honors at every examination; but in Classics only a Second, and in Philosophy and Ancient History, in spite of working thirteen hours a day for at least three weeks before, he achieved no more than a Third. But already he had won, first, a scholarship, and later, in December, 1854, had been made a " Student of Christ Church " by Doctor Pusey, one of the Canons.

A " Student " at Christ Church (known at other colleges as a " Fellow ") is a senior Member of the College engaged in teaching or research. Nowadays most of the Fellows have to spend a great deal of their time in teaching the undergraduates and lecturing to them—leaving very little opportunity to continue their own studies and produce learned books; even the tutoring and lecturing Fellows are elected only for a short time, and have to be re-elected quite frequently, while those chosen (usually by competitive examination, or as a result of their final Degree) to do research, only hold the Fellowship for a few years, and are generally not re-elected.

In Charles Dodgson's day there were a very great many Fellows who had no teaching or lecturing duties at all; they were chosen by personal knowledge rather than by examination (not a bad thing, if the chooser is honest and reliable, and really knows the candidate), and held the Fellowship for life. This supplied them with rooms in college and just enough money to live comfortably—without ever doing another stroke of work! Of course, very few of the Fellows abused their position—but a number (of whom Charles Dodgson was *not* one) tended to take things very easily. Dodgson himself pointed out the dangers of the system: " Practically, then, you examine a man at the beginning of his career . . . And what guarantee have you that he *retains* the knowledge for which you have rewarded him—beforehand ! " This is an even greater danger when the Fellowships are won by examination—and of Competitive Examinations, particularly as they came to be considered more and more as the main object of the Oxford education, Dodgson wrote even more scathingly, saying that beneath their " deadly shade all the original genius, all the exhaustive research, all the untiring life-long diligence by which our fore-fathers have so advanced human knowledge, must slowly but surely wither away, and give place to a system of Cookery in which the human mind is a sausage, and all we ask is, how much indigestible stuff can be crammed into it ? "

Dodgson, having won his Studentship (and it was not a case of favouritism by Dr. Pusey, for his name headed the list of suitable candidates), had his future assured for the rest of his life, on the conditions only that he should proceed to Holy Orders, and remain unmarried. But before settling down to his academic career, he had still other examinations to pass, first the Classics, in which he did badly and then the Mathematical Finals.

Before taking this last examination, which was to be in October, 1854, he spent the four months of the Long Vacation at Whitby in Yorkshire in company with his tutor, Professor Bartholomew Price, preparing for this final effort—with complete success, for he took a First Class Degree.

But all the time at Whitby was not spent in Mathematics. Dodgson began writing for publication during this last year as an undergraduate, for he says that two poems of his appeared in *The Oxonian Advertiser*, but " neither at all worth preservation "—and no copy seems to have survived ; and while he was staying with Professor Price, at 5, East Terrace, Whitby, a poem and a short story of his were published in *The Whitby Gazette*, both of them humorous.

The following year, having passed his "Finals" with such high honors, and become a Bachelor of Arts, he was able to devote even more time to literature—though when we consider how much Academic work he was doing, it seems almost incredible that he was able to find any freedom at all for writing. For as soon as he had taken his Degree, he began teaching private pupils and lecturing ; and before long, when he was appointed an official lecturer in Mathematics, he was lecturing for as many as seven hours a day. And to add to this work, he was also made Sub-Librarian of the College Library on February 15, 1855, which post he continued to hold until February, 1857, when he took his Master of Arts Degree.

It was, of course, only during term time that Dodgson was so extremely busy, and in the Vacations he was now able to make a serious beginning of the literary career which he wished to develop alongside his Academic work. And a beginning was readily made for him by his cousin Charles Smedley, an author of some repute in his own day, who was a regular contributor to a new humorous weekly paper called *The Comic Times* which was started in August, 1855, as a rival to *Punch*. It can hardly be described as a *serious* rival, and it did not last for much more than three months— but in it appeared at least one poem by Dodgson, the parody

THE DEAR GAZELLE.

arranged with variations

espressivo

"I never loved a dear gazelle,"
Nor aught beside that cost me much;
High prices profit those who sell.
But why should I be fond of such?

p.p   *cres:*

"To glad me with his soft black eyes,"
My infant son, from Tooting School,
Thrashed by his bigger playmate, flies,
And serve him right, the little fool!

con spirito

A Tempo

"But when he came to know me well,"
He kicked me out, her testy sire;
And when I stained my hair, that Bell
Might note the change, and thus admire

dim   *cadenza*   *D.C.*

"And love me, it was sure to die"
A muddy green, or staring blue,
While one might trace, with half an eye,
The still triumphant carrot through.

con dolore

A POEM FROM *MISCH-MASCH*

32

beginning "I never loved a dear gazelle," which was included many years later in *Rhyme and Reason*.

Meanwhile, he was editing another—the last—of his home magazines. This one, *Misch-Masch* (which is the German for "Hotch-potch"), began as usual in manuscript, but as it went on it became more and more of a scrap-book, with poems, stories, and even reviews cut out of newspapers or magazines, and pasted into the volume. The early magazines are interesting and contain much that is amusing, though on the whole they do not suggest the authorship of a very great writer. But in *Misch-Masch* Charles Dodgson begins to write like his real and famous self : and indeed early forms of poems afterwards used by him in the *Alice* books are included in it; while quite a number of other poems still live a joyous life by reason of their own excellence, besides giving us a few more side-lights on the doings at Croft. There is, for example, that doleful parody of an old ballad, "The Two Brothers," concerning two of the Dodgson boys who went out fishing one day ; the eldest began to prepare :

"He has fitted together two joints of his rod,
 And to them he has added another,
And then a great hook he took from his book,
 And ran it right into his brother."

Such a mischance, experienced by most young fishermen, probably formed the true foundation for this historical romance ; but the next verse shows Charles's imagination developing the logical possibilities in the way in which he afterwards became such an expert :

"Oh much is the noise that is made among boys
 When playfully pelting a pig,
But a far greater pother was made by his brother
 When flung from the top of the brigg."

The elder brother sits happily on the bridge-side, using the younger as bait, and he replies to the younger's complaints with a series of heartless puns :

" I am sure that our state's very nearly alike,
　　(Not considering question of slaughter)
For I have my perch on the top of the bridge,
　　And you have your perch in the water.

I stick to my perch and your perch sticks to you,
　　We are really extremely alike ;
I've a turn-pike up here, and I very much fear
　　You may soon have a turn with a pike."

The conversation goes on in this manner for some time, until one of the sisters comes out to see what is going on. She asks the elder brother what the bait is on his hook, and after a couple of fatuous answers in the ballad-style, the truth comes out :

" ' Oh what bait's that upon your hook
　　Dear brother tell to me ? '
' It is my younger brother,' he cried,
　　' Oh woe and dole is me ! ' "

And the poem ends with a sudden descent into the ridiculous and the ordinary :

" She turned herself right round about,
　　And her heart broke into three,
Said, ' One of the two will be wet through,
　　And t'other be late for his tea ! ' "

Another amusing item in *Misch-Masch* (it first appeared in some paper or other, but was not reprinted by Dodgson) is called " Hints for Etiquette ; or, Dining Out Made Easy," which contains such choice pieces of advice as :
　　" In proceeding to the dining room, the gentleman gives one arm to the lady he escorts—it is unusual to offer both . . . "
　　" To use a fork with your soup, intimating at the same

34

time to your hostess that you are reserving the spoon for the beefsteaks, is a practice wholly exploded . . . "

" The method of helping roast turkey with two carving forks is practicable, but deficient in grace . . . "

Although Dodgson himself was a most careful and polite host, his methods of carving a joint seem never to have got much beyond the " two carving forks "; one of his friends described how he volunteered to carve for them at lunch one day : " His offer was gladly accepted, but the appearance of a rather diminutive piece of neck of mutton was somewhat of a puzzle to him. He had evidently never seen such a joint in his life before, and he had frankly to confess that he did not know how to set about carving it. Directions only made things worse, and he bravely cut it to pieces in entirely the wrong fashion," and was at length left gazing wistfully at the mangled remains !

One poem pasted into *Misch-Masch*, which is reprinted in *Phantasmagoria*, " The Three Voices," appeared first in a magazine called *The Train*; for when *The Comic Times* changed hands in November, 1855, Dodgson and nearly all the contributors left it and founded this new magazine, of which the first number appeared on January 1, 1856. They were a cheery, friendly crowd, the contributors to *The Train*, headed by Edmund Yates, later a famous editor of far better known magazines such as *Once a Week*; and quiet Charles Dodgson must have found them rather overpowering. He was not a very constant contributor, only eight items by him appearing in the two years that it ran; but Yates thought very highly of his work, and one or two of Dodgson's poems—the humorous ones—are amongst his most famous. One, " *Upon the Lonely Moor*," is the first version of the " Aged, Aged Man," of which many verses remain almost unchanged; and another is " Hiawatha's Photographing," a parody of Longfellow, which is included in all the collections of Lewis Carroll's verse.

Now, even the contributions to *The Whitby Gazette* had not been signed with Charles Dodgson's real name, but appeared over the initials " B.B." ; and when he began to write and publish regularly, he felt it necessary to have some name to disguise his own. For the staid and studious Mr. Dodgson, Mathematical Lecturer at Christ Church in the University of Oxford, did not feel that it would be quite right to be known as the author of light and humorous fiction, or even of serious poetry. The writings of the other Professors and Fellows were all of a serious and academic nature—and surely they would frown upon him and consider him a most suspicious character if his name should happen to become known as a writer of nonsense literature !

So he sent to Edmund Yates a selection of possible " pen-names," beginning with " Dares," the first half of Daresbury, his birthplace ; going on to anagrams of his first two names, Charles Lutwidge—Edgar Cuthwellis and Edgar U. C. Westhall ; and finishing with translations of the same names, first into Latin as Carolus Ludovicus, and then back into other English forms Carroll and Louis or Lewis—from all of which Yates chose the name " Lewis Carroll," which was first used in the number of *The Train* for March, 1856, at the end of Dodgson's serious poem called " Solitude."

The new author " Lewis Carroll " did not desert Oxford on account of his ready admission into the exciting world of literary London : on the contrary, shortly after *The Train* reached its terminus, he began sending poems and verses to the University magazine (which also at first welcomed contributions from Cambridge) called *College Rhymes*, and even became editor for a short time, writing a few serious poems for it, and a number of burlesques which seem mainly to make fun of the usual kind of love-poetry, as in " My Fancy," which ends delightfully with this description of the poet's lady-love :

" She has the bear's ethereal grace,
 The bland hyena's laugh,
The footstep of the elephant,
 The neck of the giraffe ;
I love her still, believe me,
 Though my heart its passion hides ;
' She's all my fancy painted her,'—
 But oh ! *how much besides* ! "

This new beginning of a second career for Charles
Dodgson did not make him neglect his Academic duties in
the slightest. At the same time as he was writing Parodies
for *College Rhymes* he was also preparing erudite Mathematical works, the first of which, *A Syllabus of Plane Algebraical
Geometry . . . . by Charles Lutwidge Dodgson, M.A., Student
and Mathematical Lecturer of Christ Church, Oxford*, was
published in 1860, and was followed by quite a collection
of books and editions even duller to the ordinary reader,
though Mathematicians at the time treated them with great
respect.

Also, he was lecturing during term time, and for a few
years at least taking private pupils—though it does not seem
that he was very successful in either of these things—not
at least where undergraduates were concerned, for in after
years he proved himself excellent at teaching Logic in the
Oxford High School for girls, and even at some of the
women's colleges which were founded near the end of his
life. But as a University lecturer and tutor he was very
nearly a failure, as Mr. A. S. Russell, a more recent Mathematician, tells us : " I asked one of [his former pupils, if
Dodgson's] lectures were bad : he said they were as dull
as ditchwater. I asked another if he was a poor tutor.
He said that he and others once signed a round-robin to
the head of the college, asking to be transferred to other
hands. Dodgson himself probably realised his deficiencies

here, for though his tutorial duties were slight, he gave them up before he was fifty."

Dodgson certainly did very little tutoring ; but however badly it was done, it was not performed *quite* in the way that he described it in a letter to a brother and sister of his, Henrietta and Edwin, in 1855 :

" My one pupil has begun to work with me, and I will give you a description how the lecture is conducted. It is the most important point, you know, that the tutor should be *dignified* and at a distance from the pupil, and that the pupil should be as much as possible *degraded*. Otherwise, you know, they are not humble enough. So I sit at the further end of the room ; outside the door (*which is shut*) sits the scout ; outside the outer door (*also shut*) sits the sub-scout ; half-way down-stairs sits the sub-sub-scout ; and down in the yard sits the *pupil*.

" The questions are shouted from one to the other, and the answers come back in the same way—it is rather confusing till you are well used to it. The lecture goes on something like this :

Tutor : What is twice three ?
Scout : What's a rice-tree ?
Sub-Scout : When is ice free ?
Sub-sub-Scout : What's a nice fee ?
Pupil (*timidly*) : Half a guinea !
Sub-sub-Scout : Can't forge any !
Sub-Scout : Ho for Jinny !
Scout : Don't be a ninny !
Tutor : (*Looks offended, but tries another question*) . . . ."

To continue as Student and Lecturer at Christ Church Charles Dodgson had, besides remaining unmarried, to take Holy Orders. As far as the last of these conditions was concerned, he put it off for a few years for various reasons, not considering himself worthy or suitable to become a parson. For in spite of being truly and deeply religious— perhaps because of so being—he found so many faults in himself that he would not agree to be ordained until 1861, when his friends Dr. Pusey and Dr. Liddon over-ruled his diffidence. One reason against taking orders was his love of the Theatre—and in those days hardly any clergyman would even enter a theatre, far less make friends with an actress! Dodgson, however, was a keen play-goer, and many of his child-friends were child-actresses whom he had first met after seeing them perform on the stage. By the end of his life few people saw anything particularly wrong in knowing actors and actresses, but when Dodgson was young, all people connected with the theatre were thought to be wicked and immoral.

And another reason why Dodgson was not anxious to become a parson was that he was very shy and had a rather annoying stammer, which made preaching a difficult and trying ordeal for him. He did preach occasionally, and his extreme earnestness helped him to speak clearly and without much hesitation ; but for all that, he chose to become only a Deacon, which meant that he did not have to be a parish priest and preach regularly—though of course it was now quite correct to address him as " The Reverend C. L. Dodgson."

Lots of us are shy, particularly when we are young— most of all in the very early " grown-up " stage ; but very few, fortunately for themselves, stammer as well. But those who do, know what a terrible burden it is, and how dreadfully it cuts one off from other people. It is not recorded when Charles began to stammer, nor how it affected him at home, nor whether he was teased about it at school (which would have made it worse). But certainly he was stammering by the time he came to Oxford; and though it became less bad later, he never cured it completely—and even near the end of his life his child-friends always noticed how badly he began to stammer as soon as they met any of his grown-up acquaintances. For all his life Dodgson was rather a shy person; he was very reserved; he was very easily hurt, and very apt to see a slight where no such thing was intended: all of which things form the vicious circle from which the stammerer can so seldom escape. Thus, when he came to Oxford, he took little part in the ordinary life of the undergraduates (not even having the common ground of games to break down the barrier between him and his contemporaries), and felt little sympathy with them or their outlook—felt perhaps an antagonism for so much in which he could not, or dared not, join. The terror of being laughed at, imitated, or "snubbed" was another result of the stammer and the consequent sensitiveness which kept him so much apart from the ordinary life of young men of his own age—kept him even more from young women, of whom he might well feel far shyer, in whose company far more awkward and ludicrous—which, of course, the society of his own brothers and sisters did nothing to cure.

As an undergraduate Charles's sense of duty would have prevented him from indulging in what he must have considered the needless extravagance of big social gatherings—dinners or dances—in Oxford or London, as he was still living on his father's money. But by the time he had settled down to work as a Student, Lecturer and Tutor, his income was amply sufficient to allow him to indulge in all such pleasures—if he had inclined to do so; just as, a little later, his very good income as an author would have made it quite easy for him to marry, even if he was forced by so doing to give up his studentship, and did not feel inclined to attempt the duties of a parish priest.

But for Charles Dodgson these questions scarcely arose—and if they did so in any form, it was only at the time of the failure of his one love-affair. This, if it happened at all (for no details survive), happened when he was somewhere between the ages of twenty and thirty, when he fell in love with some girl and perhaps even asked her to marry him. If he did so, she certainly refused him—and it is even possible that he loved from afar and never dared to propose. In either case, this would have increased his feeling of diffidence, made him more desperately lonely, more anxious to escape from the troublesome passions and concerns of normal life—and in so doing have prevented him ever from becoming free of his stammer and his shyness.

It was probably many of these facts that made " Lewis Carroll " ; a different way of life might have turned his genius in other directions, perhaps leading him to even higher achievements—it is impossible to tell.

But as things were, he was bound to find himself very much isolated from the world in which most young men move, and in consequence to seek for the companionship which would give him the greatest freedom from his disabilities. And this he found in the company of children : for with children he never stammered (except when another grown-up was present), and only with them could he be quite and delightfully at his ease. Nearly all the child-friends who have written of their memories of Lewis Carroll tell us how natural and unself-conscious he was when alone with them, and how completely his stammer vanished away. Why this was so, it is not easy to say for certain, and how generally true, it is even more impossible to tell—though one other stammerer at least can bear testimony to exactly

41

the same experience of perfect freedom when in company with children, and to the consequent longing for their company more and more, to the exclusion of his own contemporaries, together with the ability to identify himself (for the time being) with the children, and to be considered by them in the position of a child rather than as a grown-up.

Such an unusual state of things as this does not continue once the sufferer is able to break the vicious circle of his own shyness, stammering, and general fear of the normal contacts of life—though it may leave an ability to enter into childhood again such as most people do not possess.

Dodgson, however, never escaped completely—and almost to the end of his life he was still making friends with children and delighting in their society far rather than in that of anyone else.

Already in his early Oxford years he was beginning to form these friendships—indeed, there was hardly any " beginning," for his own youngest brothers and sisters were still children at least when he began to compile *Misch-Masch* for their benefit.

But who his first children-friends were outside his own family, it is not possible to say for certain—whether they were the children of Tennyson, the Poet Laureate, of George MacDonald, or of Dean Liddell.

Early in 1859 he went to visit Tennyson at his home in the Isle of Wight—and found the great poet busily mowing his front lawn. Tennyson took him over the house, finishing with " the nursery, where we found the beautiful little Hallam (his son), who remembered me more readily than his father had done . . . I lunched with them the next day, but saw very little of Tennyson himself, and afterwards showed the photographs to Mrs. Tennyson and the children, not omitting to get Hallam's autograph in a large, bold, text-hand, under his portrait. The children insisted on reading out the poetry opposite to the pictures, and when

42

they came to their father's portrait (which has for a motto ' The Poet in a golden clime was born,' etc.) Lionel puzzled over it for a moment, and then began, boldly ' The Pope—! ', on which Mrs. Tennyson began laughing . . . . " (Perhaps nearly thirty years later Dodgson remembered this when he made his Mad Gardener sing : " He thought he saw an argument That proved it was the Pope ! ").

From what Dodgson says in this letter (which was written in May, 1859, to his cousin William), he must have made friends with the Tennyson boys at some time before this visit : and certainly he kept up his friendship with them for a number of years afterwards.

Charles Dodgson did not usually care for little boys— but there were a number of exceptions to this rule— beginning with Hallam and Lionel Tennyson, and going on to at least one of the next group of early child-friends— Greville MacDonald.

Greville's father was George MacDonald, who wrote such delightful fairy romances as *The Princess and the Goblin* ; and Dodgson first met him in 1857 while he was having treatment for his stammer from a well known doctor and philologist called James Hunt. Dodgson's stammer was not cured by this excellent man, but George MacDonald was introduced by him, and was soon on friendly terms.

But it was not until a couple of years later that Dodgson first met the MacDonald children, the second and third of whom were Mary and Greville. He was in town one afternoon, and went to visit another acquaintance, the sculptor Alexander Munro ; and there he found the two children— with Greville " posing " as the boy riding a dolphin which may still be seen in Hyde Park ; and he wrote in his diary of that day : " They were a girl and a boy, about seven and six years old [they were actually a year or more younger]— I claimed their acquaintance, and began at once proving to the boy, Greville, that he had better take the opportunity of having his head changed for a marble one. The effect was that in about two minutes they had entirely forgotten that I was a total stranger, and were earnestly arguing the question as if we were old acquaintances." Dodgson pointed out that a marble head would not need to be brushed and combed, and Greville seemed most impressed, for he wore his hair long, as boys did in those days: "Do you hear *that* Mary?" he said triumphantly, "It needn't be combed!" And Dodgson goes on: "I have no doubt combing, with his great head of long hair, like Hallam Tennyson's, *was* the misery of his life. His final argument was that a marble head couldn't speak, and as I couldn't convince either that he would be all the better for that, I gave in."

The friendship, so well begun, continued for a number of years, and Greville writes that "our annual treat was Uncle Dodgson taking us to the Polytechnic for the entrancing 'dissolving views' of fairy tales, or to go down in the diving bell, or watch the mechanical athlete *Leotard*. There was also the Coliseum in Albany Street, with its storms by land and sea on a wonderful stage, and its great panorama of London." This, of course, was in the days very long before the invention of cinemas, and such "scenic effects" as Greville describes were the most that could be offered instead. Simpler amusements were the toy shops—"not to mention bath buns and ginger beer"—and Greville also remembered from the very early days an occasion when he leant against "Uncle Dodgson's knee as he drew for me in my copy-book . . . a picture that evoked from us shrieks of delight. In the far distance was a train steaming away from its station to negotiate a humpy railway bridge. In the foreground a very stout perspiring gentleman was mopping his head with one hand, while his wife, scraggy and grim, dragged him along by the other and shouted at him:

' It's puffing away fit to burst itself; we shall lose it, John, if you don't run faster! ' " . . . And he had already drawn a delightful picture of the first meeting, showing Greville in his kilt, holding the marble head, and Mr. Munro rushing away in terror with his hair and beard standing on end.

A little while later he was writing letters to Mary MacDonald:

" It's been so frightfully hot here that I've been almost too weak to hold a pen, and even if I had been able, there was no ink—it had all evaporated into a cloud of black steam, and in that state it has been floating about the room, inking the walls and ceiling, till they're hardly fit to be seen . . . . " Or like this : " . . . . do not suppose I didn't *write*, hundreds of times ; the difficulty has been with the *directing*—I directed the letters so violently at first, that they went far beyond the mark—some of them were picked up at the other end of Russia. Last week I made a very near shot, and actually succeeded in putting ' Earl's Terrace, Kensington,' only I overdid the number, and put 12000, instead of 12. If you enquire for the letter at No. 12000, I dare say they'll give it you. After that, I fell into a feeble state of health, and directed the letters so gently that one of them only reached the other side of the room . . ."

Or in the form of a nonsense-story: " Once upon a time there was a little girl, and she had a cross old Uncle . . . Well, . . . the poor old Uncle's nose kept getting longer and longer, and his temper getting shorter and shorter, and post after post went by, and no sonnet came—I leave off here to explain how they sent letters in those days : there were no gates, so the gate-posts weren't obliged to stay in one place—consequence of which, they went wandering all over the country—consequence of which, if you wanted to send a letter anywhere, all you had to do was to fasten it on to a gate-post that was going in the proper direction—(only they sometimes changed their minds, which was awkward)

—This was called ' Sending a letter by the post.' They did things very simply in those days : if you had a lot of money, you just dug a hole under the hedge, and popped it in : then you said you had ' put it in the bank,' and you felt quite comfortable about it. And the way they travelled was—there were railings all along the side of the road, and they used to get up, and walk along the top, as steadily as they could, till they tumbled off—which they mostly did very soon—this was called ' travelling by rail ' . . . "

And so we see Charles Dodgson settled at Christ Church, already beginning to make friends with children and invent stories—already needing the escape that such friendships and such stories held for him. We see him as the rather dull and learned Mathematics tutor, failing to find any real friendship among his fellow Dons, making the acquaintance of famous writers and artists—Tennyson, Rossetti, Ruskin, George MacDonald, Arthur Hughes, to name only a few— but never being on real terms of intimacy with any of them ; we see him shy, retiring, lonely—cut off by these causes and by the stammer which itself formed the keystone in this arch of unfortunate handicaps—seeking more and more surely for the companionship of children as he found that only among them could he be completely at his ease and escape completely from the dark shadow of his own real and fancied disabilities.

And so the scene is set for the first appearance of Alice.

CHAPTER IV

ALICE'S ADVENTURES

IN 1855, when Charles Dodgson had only lately taken his degree as Bachelor of Arts, a new Dean (as the head of Christ Church is called) was appointed—Henry George Liddell, part author of the famous Greek Lexicon known as " Liddell and Scott "—and before very long Dodgson and he became well acquainted.

Dean Liddell had a number of children, but the three eldest girls, Lorina, Alice and Edith, are the ones who concern us most. Dodgson began to make friends with them in 1859 or thereabouts, when Lorina was eight, Alice six and Edith four. Perhaps as he sat in the Librarian's room looking out over the Deanery garden, he may have seen the three little girls playing there—but he is not likely to have known them at that time, for when he ceased to be Sub-Librarian at the beginning of 1857, even Lorina was only six years old.

But as time went on Dodgson became a great friend of the three little girls, who went often to visit him, accompanied by their governess, Miss Prickett. In those days he lived in an old building overlooking the meadows, which was pulled down only a few years later, when he moved into the great quadrangle—" Tom Quad " it is called, after the bell in the little tower over the gateway, who is " Big Tom." It was up many flights of stairs to Mr. Dodgson's rooms, and there was a view over the meadows to the river in the distance, and the little mill stream flowing down to join it.

Dodgson of course called sometimes at the Deanery, and there, besides the children, he made the acquaintance of Dinah, the tabby cat. She was given to Lorina, but before long became Alice's special pet; the children also had canaries—but they never had a white rabbit! In the summer he would teach the little girls to play croquet in the quiet Deanery garden—and summer and winter alike, he was always ready to tell stories or draw pictures.

During the long summer vacation of nearly four months the whole Liddell family went away from Oxford to a house which the Dean had built near Llandudno in North Wales, looking out over the sea, past the big rocky headland called the Great Orme's Head to the more distant island of Anglesey and the entrance to the Menai Straits. This house was called "Penmorfa," and there many people used to visit the Liddells—including Charles Dodgson at least once.

Another visitor a year or two later than Dodgson (who must have been there about 1860) was the artist W. B. Richmond, who painted a picture of the three little girls, and who has described the place : " This house . . . stood in surroundings of surpassing loveliness close by the shore at the south-west corner of the Great Orme's Head. Behind it rose the wild headland, before it lay an expanse of shallow sea, so that when the tide was out and the sun set over the island, wondrous colors were thrown upon the rugged hills and reflected in glittering lights and tints upon the wet sands. In this romantic spot the happy days were spent in picnics, drives, and sketching, in merry scrambles over the hills in the blazing sunshine, or sometimes, when the day had been too hot, and the moon was full, a long and enchanting expedition was made by moonlight through a silver, shimmering, mysterious land."

Here, and in Oxford again, Dodgson continued telling stories to the three little girls, and drawing pictures for them—but alas, none of these have survived, for who could have guessed that the quiet, shy Mr. Dodgson who took such an odd pleasure in amusing the children was to become so famous an author !

"We never went to tea with him," said Alice Liddell nearly seventy years later when trying to recall her child-

ALICE LIDDELL
Photograph by Charles Dodgson

hood, "nor did he come to tea with us " (afternoon tea had not been invented in 1860, though ten years later it had become quite the rule). "He used sometimes to come to the Deanery on the afternoons when we had a half-holiday . . . When we went on the river for the afternoon with Mr. Dodgson, which happened at most four or five times every summer term, he always brought out with him a large basket full of cakes, and a kettle, which we used to boil under a haycock, if we could find one . . . The party usually consisted of five—one of Mr. Dodgson's men friends as well as himself and us three. His brother occasionally took an oar in the merry party, but our most usual fifth was Mr. Duckworth, who sang well. On our way back we generally sang songs popular at the time, such as 'Star of the evening, beautiful star,' and 'Twinkle, twinkle, little star,' and 'Will you walk into my parlour, said the spider to the fly' . . . On one occasion two of Mr. Dodgson's sisters joined the party, making seven of us, all in one boat. They seemed to us rather stout, and one might have expected that, with such a load in it, the boat would have been swamped. However, it was not the river that swamped us, but the rain. It came on to pour so hard that we had to land at Iffley, and after trying to dry the Misses Dodgson at a fire, we drove home . . ."

On more usual boating parties the children were taught to row, and a particular treat was to steer the boat.

How delightful such afternoons must have been : to get away altogether from the governess and the special teachers who were hired for " extras " such as French, German and Art—even to get away from dancing lessons, where the most difficult dance was the old-fashioned " Quadrille " ; to escape from Miss Prickett's rather dreary lessons in history—from dull books with names like *Magnall's Questions* or *Mrs. Markham's History*—where uninteresting facts about Edgar Atheling or Edwin and Morcar were to be found. To escape from the " improving " poetry of Isaac Watts and Robert Southey was also a great relief—for with other grown-ups less sensible than Mr. Dodgson

We lived beneath the mat
Warm and snug and fat
But one woe, & that
Was the cat!
To our joys
a clog, In
our eyes a
fog, On our
hearts a log
Was the dog!
When the
Cat's away,
Then
the mice
will
play,
But, alas!
one day, (So they say)
Came the dog and
cat, Hunting
for a
rat,
Crushed
the mice
all flat,
Each
one
as
he
sat
Underneath the mat, Warm & snug, & fat - Think of that!

"THE MOUSE'S TAIL"
From *Alice's Adventures Underground*

one would so often be asked to recite such a poem as—
> " How doth the little busy bee
> Improve each shining hour
> And gather honey all the day
> From every opening flower.
>
> How skilfully she builds her cell !
> How neat she spreads the wax !
> And labours hard to store it well
> With the sweet food she makes . . ."

or the even duller and longer one by Southey which begins—
> " ' You are old, Father William,' the young man cried,
> ' The few locks which are left you are grey ;
> You are hale, Father William, a hearty old man,
> Now tell me the reason, I pray '."
> ' In the days of my youth,' Father William replied,
> I remembered that youth would fly fast,
> And abused not my health and my vigour at first,
> That I never might need them at last . . .' "

or again that quite unheard of, and most unpleasantly morbid poem by a certain G. W. Langford, which is made up of many such verses as—
> " Speak gently to your little child,
> Its love be sure to gain ;
> Teach it in accents soft and mild—
> It may not long remain ! "

And on a picnic one's manners did not have to be quite so perfect as was usually expected—certainly no one was expected to curtsey !

For usually there was only one grown-up on a river picnic, besides Mr. Dodgson—and in most cases that one seems to have been the Rev. Robinson Duckworth who was a Fellow and Tutor at Trinity College from 1860 to 1866, and in later years became Canon of Westminster. Dodgson may have known Duckworth when they were boys, for

Duckworth, only two years younger than he, was born at Liverpool which is not so very far from Daresbury. However, at Oxford they became friends—as much, that is, as Dodgson could form a real friendship with anyone—and he was usually asked to make the fifth on the river-picnics, and a number of such notes as this would be sent to Trinity :

"Dear Duckworth, will you dine with me in Hall on Thursday? Or on Saturday? And should you be disposed any day soon for a row on the river for which I could secure some Liddells as companions? . . ."

Or even more shortly :

"Dear Duckworth, could you help row my friends on Wednesday? Truly yours, C. L. Dodgson."

Perhaps this was the invitation for the particular picnic which has become so famous—or perhaps merely for an ordinary day ; for, as Dodgson himself wrote some years after :

"Many a day had we rowed together on that quiet stream —the three little maidens and I—and many a fairy tale had been extemporised for their benefit whether it were at times when the narrator was "i' the vein," and fancies unsought came crowding thick upon him, or at times when the jaded Muse was goaded into action, and plodded meekly on, more because she had to say something than that she had something to say—yet none of these many tales got written down : they lived and died, like summer midges, each in its own golden afternoon until there came a day when, as it chanced, one of my little listeners petitioned that the tale might be written out for her . . ."

That "golden afternoon" was July 4, 1862, a day of perfect summer lying like the gentle white heat haze over the quiet grey and yellow of the ancient city of Oxford— quiet, for the Long Vacation had begun, and in those days the grass grew between the cobbles of the High Street before the next term began in distant October—quiet, for besides the University there was very little city, a few shops in the center, a number of poorer houses in St. Ebbe's parish where the river Thames sweeps round between Folly Bridge beyond Christ Church and the old Castle tower near where the station now is, and perhaps a few, a very few big houses in " North Oxford " where the Professors —the only married members of the University—lived ; there were open fields within a few minutes' walk of every point in Oxford then, fields stretching away to the little lonely villages of Iffley and Cowley and Headington, to Summertown where Burne-Jones went as an under-graduate to paint apple-blossom, to Botley or Hinksey, all of which are now joined to Oxford in a vast, clinging mass of suburb and factory.

The three little girls on that distant afternoon came tripping happily forth from the Deanery in their white cotton dresses, openwork socks, black shoes, and white hats, and were met by Mr. Dodgson and Mr. Duckworth, both dressed in white flannel trousers, the black top-hat of the clergyman exchanged for a white straw " boater "—but in black boots still, for white canvas shoes had not then been invented.

Out they went into the meadow that runs down to the river, across the little mill stream (most of which is now an underground drain through which it is just possible to float in a canoe—a punt will not fit round the corners), and on to the road leading to Folly Bridge : St. Aldate's (which the older Oxford people still pronounce " St. Olds "), the street with the little shop (No. 83), "—a little dark shop, full of all manner of curious things," in which the old Sheep sits in *Through the Looking-Glass*. At Folly Bridge they hired a rowing boat and turned up the river, Duckworth rowing stroke and Dodgson rowing bow. Usually they went down the river towards Iffley—and this must have been a particular occasion, for Dodgson wrote in his diary that day, " I

54

made an expedition *up* the river to Godstow with the three Liddells . . .", underlining "*up*" as if to point out how unusual it was.

They rowed away past the little houses of St. Ebbe's, past the old castle tower, and away into the country between the green meadows and the hayfields, until they could see the towers and spires of Oxford gleaming and shimmering behind them like honey-gold embroidered on the blueness of the sky. The river wound on, broad still and leisurely, the tall willow trees reflected in the water, the cows plodding peacefully through the shallows at the edge, and perhaps one farmer striding down the tow-path and shouting a cheery " good day "—the only passer-by on such an afternoon. Years afterwards Dodgson wrote that he could remember that afternoon " almost as clearly as if it were yesterday—the cloudless blue above, the watery mirror below, the boat drifting idly on its way, the tinkle of the drops that fell from the oars, as they waved so sleepily to and fro, and (the one bright gleam of life in all the slumberous scene) the three eager faces, hungry for fairyland, and who would not be said ' nay ' to : from whose lips ' Tell us a story, please,' had all the stern immutability of Fate ! . . . I distinctly remember . . . how, in a desperate attempt to strike out some new line of fairy-lore, I sent my heroine straight down a rabbit hole, to begin with, without the least idea what was to happen afterwards."

Duckworth listened with almost as much delight, and more amazement than the children.

" Dodgson," said he presently, " is this an extempore romance of yours ? " And Dodgson replied : " Yes, I'm inventing as we go along."

Presently a bend of the river brought in sight the gray ruins of Gostow Nunnery, and the extreme heat of the afternoon did not encourage them to go any further. They landed on the grassy bank and sought the shelter of a nearby haystack ; here the picnic basket was unpacked, the kettle boiled—and Dodgson was pestered to go on with the story.

" Sometimes, to tease us—and perhaps being really tired," said Alice long afterwards when telling the history of that day, " Mr. Dodgson would stop suddenly and say : ' And that's all till next time.' ' Ah, but it is next time,' would be·the exclamation from all three ; and after some persuasion the story would start afresh."

There was no need that day to shelter from the rain in a cottage with a fire to dry their clothes as on the occasion when Dodgson's sisters were of the party, but when he first wrote down the story he remembered that cottage and that fire, so probably he brought it into the story as he told it, just to make it more real. For a number of the characters were real people : Alice was the heroine, of course ; but Lorina and Edith were there too—as the Lory and the Eaglet —and there was Mr. Duckworth as the Duck and even Dodgson himself, disguised as the Dodo (for the children must often have heard him telling strange grown-ups that his name was " Do-Do-Dodgson ").

It was late when they got back to Christ Church that evening—at least half-past eight—but it had been a truly memorable day for them all ; and as the children said good-night, Alice turned suddenly and exclaimed : " Oh, Mr. Dodgson, I wish you would write out Alice's adventures for me ! " And Dodgson promised that he would, and even sat up most of that night jotting down on paper all that he could remember of the story.

And when he had time, he wrote it out for Alice in his beautiful neat hand—even neater than when he had written the family magazines for his own brothers and sisters— and he drew pictures for the book, though he had never had a drawing lesson in his life, and wrote in the front of it : " A Christmas Gift to a Dear Child in Memory of a Summer Day," and at the end stuck in a little photograph which he had taken of Alice Liddell, the bright, rather quaint little girl with almost straight dark hair cut in a fringe across her forehead, and the " dreaming eyes of wonder." He meant it to be ready for Christmas—but it was February, 1863, before he could hand it in triumphantly at the Deanery.

It was called *Alice's Adventures Underground,* and is not much more than half as long as the book which he finally made out of it—and it had a few passages in it, and a poem or two, which you will not find in the real *Alice in Wonderland.*

There is, for example, the episode which was suggested by the disastrous picnic in the rain. It begins after the Mouse's history lesson (was the Mouse one of the Miss Dodgsons?):

" . . . How are you getting on now dear? " said the Mouse, turning to Alice as it spoke.

" As well as ever," said poor Alice, " it doesn't seem to dry me at all."

" In that case," said the Dodo solemnly, rising to his feet, " I move that the meeting adjourn, for the immediate adoption of more energetic remedies—"

" Speak English! " said the Duck. " I don't know the meaning of half those long words, and what's more, I don't believe you do either! " Some of the other birds tittered audibly.

" I only meant to say," said the Dodo in a rather offended voice, " that I know of a house near here, where we could get the young lady and the rest of the party dried, and then we could listen comfortably to the story which I think you were good enough to promise to tell us," bowing gravely to the Mouse.

The Mouse made no objection to this, and the whole party moved along the river bank (for the pool had by this time begun to flow out of the hall, and the edge of it was fringed with rushes and forget-me-nots) in a slow procession, the Dodo leading the way. After a time the Dodo became impatient, and, leaving the Duck to bring up the rest of the party, moved on at a quicker pace with Alice, the Lory, and the Eaglet, and soon brought them to a little cottage, and there they sat snugly by the fire, wrapped up in blankets, until the rest of the party had arrived, and they were all dry again.

Then they all sat down again in a large ring on the bank, and begged the Mouse to begin his story.

" Mine is a long and sad tale ! " said the mouse . . ."

If you look for this passage in Chapter III of *Alice in Wonderland*, you will find that in its place is the very much more amusing account of the " Caucus Race " ; and there are other touches in the original story as it was first written out for Alice Liddell which were more personal when intended only for the children at the Deanery. When Alice mentions Dinah, for example, and all the birds and animals run away in terror, she goes on to talk to herself :

" I do wish some of them had stayed a little longer ! And I was getting to be such friends with them—really the Lory and I were almost like sisters, and so was that dear little Eaglet ! And then the Duck and the Dodo ! How nicely the Duck sang to us as we came along through the water : and if the Dodo hadn't known the way to that nice little cottage, I don't know when we should have got dry again—".

And in Alice's own copy of the story there were very big bits missing which Dodgson wrote in afterwards ; directly after the adventure with the Wood-pigeon Alice finds the door in the tree and goes straight into the garden where the gardeners are painting the roses ; there is no Duchess in the early story, the Queen of Hearts is also the Marchioness of Mock Turtles, and she introduces Alice to the Mock-Turtle and the Gryphon—and after that, the whole trial takes only one page before Alice says : " You're nothing but a pack of cards!" and the dream comes to an end.

But Alice and her sisters were very pleased with their book, when Mr. Dodgson had finished writing it out and drawing his own pleasant, but rather unskilful illustrations for it—early in 1863. And besides showing it to their friends, they were in the habit of leaving it on the table in the Deanery drawing room for chance visitors to look at.

And one day a writer friend of Dodgson's, Henry Kingsley (whose more famous brother, Charles, was the

EDITH, LORINA AND ALICE LIDDELL.
Photograph by Lewis Carroll

author of *Westward Ho!* and *The Water Babies*) called on Dean Liddell and happened to pick up *Alice's Adventures Underground*. He liked it so much and thought it was so good and unusual, that he begged Alice and her mother to persuade Dodgson to have it published—and he also told the author that such a story should be given to all the other children in England and not merely the little Liddell girls.

But Dodgson was a very careful person, and he was always extremely doubtful of his own powers—as an author as at everything else. He decided to have a second opinion, and borrowing the manuscript from Alice, lent it to George MacDonald with the request that it should be read to his children. And when Mrs. MacDonald read the story out loud to the family, it was just as much of a success as it had been at the Deanery—more so, perhaps, for little Greville was so pleased with it that he said there " ought to be 60,000 volumes of it ! "

This was most encouraging, and Charles Dodgson at once began to re-write the story for publication, cutting out the special bits about Lorina and Edith, Mr. Duckworth and himself, polishing up what was already written, and adding a great deal more to make the book long enough to publish. He did not make up all the new material then and there, for some at least had been told to the Liddells on other picnics, or perhaps while sitting in the shady Deanery garden. There was " The Mad Tea-Party," for example, which must surely have been based on one of these earlier stories— for there are the three Liddells again in it, this time as " Elsie, Lacie and Tillie," the three little sisters who lived in a well and were learning to draw. For " Elsie " is " L.C." (for Lorina Charlotte), and " Lacie " is an anagram of Alice, and Tillie is short for Matilda, which was the nickname her sisters had invented for Edith. And the Mad Hatter was also suggested by a real person, though who he was does not seem certain ; some people say that he was Theophilus Carter who kept a furniture shop in the High ; but Dodgson's own nephew tells us that he was one of the other students or tutors at Christ Church—which seems much more likely.

And there was the whole account of the trial of the Knave of Hearts, probably made up specially for the book, with the exception of the poem " Alice's Evidence," which was altered and improved from one called " She's All My Fancy Painted Him," that must have been published in some

paper about 1855, for a cutting containing it is pasted into
Misch-Masch, where it begins :

> " She's all my fancy painted him
>   (I make no idle boast) ;
> If he or you had lost a limb,
>   Which would have suffered most ?
>
> He said that you had been to her,
>   And seen me here before ;
> But, in another character,
>   She was the same of yore.
>
> There was not one that spoke to us,
>   Of all that thronged the street ;
> So he sadly got into a 'bus,
>   And pattered with his feet."

After which, it goes on with the second verse in " Alice's
Evidence " and very little is altered. Only one poem in the
book is not by Dodgson, and that is the " accusation "
read by the White Rabbit, beginning · " The Queen of
Hearts, she made some tarts," which is in reality half of the
first verse of a longish " nonsense " poem of four verses,
each telling the fortunes of the different suits in a pack of
cards, which was first published in 1782 with no author's
name.

It must have been mainly during 1863 that Dodgson
was re-writing *Alice's Adventures Underground* and making
of it a long enough book for publication ; and he tells us
that " in writing it out I added many fresh ideas, which
seemed to grow of themselves upon the original stock . . .
but every such idea and nearly every word of the dialogue,
came of itself. Sometimes an idea comes at night, when I
have to get up and strike a light to note it down—sometimes
when out on a lonely winter walk, when I have had to stop,
and with half-frozen fingers jot down a few words which

should keep the new-born idea from perishing—but whenever or however it comes, *it comes of itself*. I cannot set invention going like a clock . . . " Dodgson was indeed fortunate that he did not have to earn his living as an author, but could pass the years in security at Christ Church, " waiting for the spark from Heaven to fall " like Matthew Arnold's Scholar Gipsy.

But when he had finished writing the complete book, early in 1864, the question of illustrations arose. Dodgson had drawn his own pictures in *Alice's Adventures Underground*—" designs that rebelled against every law of Anatomy or Art," as he described them, though he had borrowed a book of natural history from Dean Liddell in an attempt to make some figures at least as correct as he could : but in no natural history would he have found a Mock Turtle !

Dodgson consulted Mr. Duckworth, who suggested an artist called John Tenniel, whose illustrations of Æsop Dodgson would have known—besides his frequent cartoons in *Punch*—and Dodgson asked his friend Tom Taylor, a well known writer of plays, to introduce him to Tenniel, who at once agreed to supply the illustrations. An agreement was made between author and artist on April 5, and a couple of months later Dodgson in a letter to Tom Taylor, mentions his " fairy-tale which Mr. Tenniel (in consequence of your kind introduction) is now illustrating," and he goes on to ask for suggestions of a name for the book, having thought of *Alice's Adventures Underground* and *Alice's Golden Hour*, and rejected them both. The next name proposed was *Alice's Hour in Elfland*, but on June 18 (1864) he finally decided to call his book *Alice's Adventures in Wonderland*.

But the adventures of the book were by no means ended : having had a trial sheet printed at the Clarendon Press in Oxford, Dodgson entered into an agreement with Messrs. Macmillan to publish the book—but at his own risk and expense, for he himself paid the bill of £131 9s. to the

Clarendon Press for the first edition of two thousand copies.

The book was ready in the summer of 1865, and on July 4, exactly three years after the day of the picnic on which the *Adventures* had first been told, Alice Liddell received a presentation copy.

But Dodgson was not easily satisfied, and scarcely had the book been published when he decided that it was badly printed and that a new edition must be prepared instead. On August 2 he wrote in his diary: " Finally decided on the re-print of ' Alice,' and that the first 2,000 shall be sold as waste paper . . . If I make £500 by sale, this will be a loss of £100, and the loss on the first 2,000 will probably be £100, leaving me £200 out of pocket. But if a second 2,000 could be sold it would cost £300, and bring in £500, thus squaring accounts ; and any further sale would be a gain : but that I can hardly hope for."

But he was very much more than paid back, for at the time of his death eighty-six thousand copies had been sold of the 6s. edition, and seventy thousand in a cheaper edition !

In a letter (probably to Tom Taylor) written on August 3, 1865, Dodgson gives the reason for suppressing the first edition : " I write to beg that if you have received the copy I sent you of *Alice's Adventures in Wonderland* you will suspend your judgment on it till I can send you a better copy. We are printing it again as the pictures are so badly done . . ."

Only a few copies of the first edition have survived until now—and one at least of them was sold not many years ago for £5,000. But even more amazing was the sale in London in 1928 when the copy of *Alice's Adventures Underground* which Dodgson had written out for Alice Liddell was sold by auction for £15,000—the highest sum ever paid for a manuscript at a sale !

But no one dreamt of such things in the autumn of 1865 when most of the copies of the first edition were returned by their buyers to be destroyed, and the new, properly printed edition came out in early November (though dated 1866) so as to be ready for Christmas ; and Dodgson sent Alice another copy—and one also to Duckworth with the inscription : " R. Duckworth with the sincere regards of the Author, in memory of our voyage."

But for Alice Liddell the dedication was already printed in the book—the poem at the beginning whose last verse is this :

> " Alice ! A childish story take,
>   And, with a gentle hand,
> Lay it where Childhood's dreams are twined
>   In Memory's mystic band.
> Like pilgrim's wither'd wreath of flowers
>   Pluck'd in a far-off land."

CHAPTER V

THROUGH THE LOOKING-GLASS

Alice's Adventures in Wonderland appeared at the end of 1865, and was greeted kindly by most of the reviewers—though in those days very few children's books received much more than a passing mention of up to a dozen lines in an article on the new books for Christmas. There was only one important paper, *The Athenæum* (" Golly, what a paper ! " as John Finsbury says of it in *The Wrong Box*—though it was really a very good paper indeed, and usually recognised a good book !) which failed to realise that there was something out of the ordinary in *Alice* : " This is a dream story," wrote the critic, " but who can in cold blood manufacture a dream . . . ? Mr. Carroll has laboured hard to heap together strange adventures and heterogeneous combinations, and we acknowledge the hard labour . . . We fancy that any real child might be more puzzled than enchanted by this stiff, over-wrought story."

But this was not the general criticism ; and in a year or two " Mr. Lewis Carroll " became a very famous man : or rather, his *name* became famous, for few people beyond his friends knew that " Lewis Carroll " was really the " pen-name " of the Rev. Charles Dodgson the rather dull lecturer in mathematics at Christ Church ! Yet, of course, Dodgson, the real Lewis Carroll, soon realised what pleasure *Alice* was bringing to countless readers, old as well as young, and began to think of writing another story.

In after years Dodgson used never to read any of the reviews of his books, holding that if good, the review would make him proud, and if bad, it would depress him too much ;

but in his early years as an author he was quite human enough not only to read his " notices " but to cut them out and collect them in a scrap-book !

Presently the news got about that " Lewis Carroll " was writing another book, and letters from editors of magazines began to turn up on Mr. Dodgson's breakfast table (forwarded from Macmillan the publisher, for a thing which Dodgson hated particularly was to receive letters addressed to " Lewis Carroll, Esq., Christ Church " !)— begging him to allow them to publish the new story in their magazines, offering him as much as two guineas a page—a very high price indeed for a serial story in the Eighteen-Sixties.

But Dodgson, not having to earn his living by his books, went his own way, carefully and methodically, spending a great deal of time in thinking and waiting for ideas before he even began to write his new story.

He decided almost at once that it was going to be a sequel to *Alice*, and so he began to think over some others of the stories he had told the Liddell children, particularly the more recent ones told when they were slightly older than on the day of the voyage up the Thames. In the days when *Alice* was told, the three little girls spent much of their time in the Deanery garden learning to play croquet, and Dodgson must often have come to help them ; and when they could play well he even went so far as to invent a new game called " Croquet Castles " which was printed privately for him in 1863. This game was at first " for five players " —perhaps Duckworth, or even Miss Prickett the governess being included ; but soon afterwards, Dodgson had revised rules " for four players " printed. Croquet is one of the most delightful of ball games, and it is a pity that so very few people play it nowadays ; but when Alice was a girl it was the most popular game—certainly among ladies, whose skirts were far too wide and "hooped" just then for anything so violent as lawn-tennis! Dodgson invented his new version of this popular game with the help of Alice and her sisters; it is too long to describe here, and would seem dull to people who have never played any sort of croquet, but one gets an idea of how much more interest Dodgson managed to introduce into the game from the general description:

"This game requires 8 balls, 8 arches, and 4 flags; 4 of the balls are called 'soldiers' and the others 'sentinels.' The arches and flags are set up, making 4 'castles,' and each player has a castle, a soldier and a sentinel . . .", and from Rule III which runs: "If a sentinel and a soldier touch, while both are within the sentinel's castle, or if a soldier enter a castle while its sentinel and his own are both 'on duty,' the soldier becomes 'prisoner' and is placed behind the flag. He cannot move till released which is done either by his own sentinel (on duty) coming and touching the flag, or by the sentinel leaving the castle . . ." This was not, perhaps, as difficult a game to play as the Queen of Hearts' Croquet Match, where the mallets were flamingoes, the balls were hedgehogs, the arches were soldiers (very much "on duty" when the Queen became headstrong!) and instead of the smooth green turf of the Deanery lawn, "it was all in ridges and furrows" (even the use of ostriches, in the first version of the story, would not have made it much easier!)—but still, "Croquet Castles" was really too complicated for most people!

Even earlier than this, Dodgson had invented a card game called "Court Circular" which is also rather too complicated for most players; but it has no connection with *Alice*, except that Hearts are the most important suit; and the pleasantest thing about it is that Dodgson invented for his "sequences" such names as "A Sympathy—i.e., 3, or 4, Hearts"; "A Valentine—i.e., 2 Hearts"; "An Etiquette—i.e., 2 Court-cards."

But after the croquet craze, when the Liddell girls were a trifle older, came an interest in Chess—quite a difficult enough game already without any new rules invented by Dodgson—and Alice Liddell remembered in her old age that many of the chapters in *Through the Looking-Glass* were based on stories about Chess which Dodgson made up while he was teaching them to play.

The actual idea of the Looking-Glass Country, however, was suggested not by any of the Liddells but by quite a different Alice, a distant relation of his own with whom he made friends one day when he was staying with his uncle Mr. Lutwidge in his house at Onslow Square, South Kensington. At the back of the house was a big garden, and one day as Dodgson was walking there, watching some children at play, he heard one little girl called by her name " Alice." At once he went up to her and said : " So you are another Alice ! I am very fond of Alices." He talked with her for a little while, and then he said : " Will you come with me and see something which is rather puzzling ? "

Alice agreed, and followed him into the house where he gravely presented her with an orange.

" Now tell me," he said, " which hand are you holding that orange in ? "

" My right hand," replied Alice, promptly.

" Now," said Mr. Dodgson, " go and look at the little girl in the glass over there and tell me which hand *she* is holding the orange in."

Obediently Alice went and stood in front of the long mirror which hung in one corner of the room and looked carefully at her reflection.

" She is holding it in her left hand," she replied.

" How do you explain that ? " continued Mr. Dodgson.

This time Alice had to consider the problem carefully, but after a few minutes she said :

" Supposing I was on the *other* side of the glass, wouldn't the orange still be in my right hand ? "

Laughing delightfully, Mr. Dodgson exclaimed : " Well done, little Alice, it's the best answer I've had yet ! "

And ever afterwards he would say that it was this answer given by Alice Raikes that had suggested to him the thought

MARY BADCOCK (TENNIEL'S " ALICE ")

of a " Looking-Glass Country " where everything should be back-to-front.

This must have happened early in 1866, for by the end of the year Dodgson had written, or at least prepared enough of his new story to begin looking for someone to illustrate it. Naturally he turned first to John Tenniel who had made such excellent pictures for *Alice's Adventures* ; but Tenniel at first refused to illustrate another book for him. Dodgson was a very difficult author for artists to work with, insisting on the minutest details in every picture being done exactly as he wished and indeed he had almost a quarrel with Tenniel over the drawing of Alice herself. To begin with, Dodgson thought of making his heroine actually look like Alice Liddell, with dark hair and a fringe ; but he and Tenniel decided to make the Alice of the story look more like the usual little girl of the period—with long hair and a ribbon round it. (You may find pictures in stories of the "Sixties" that might almost have come from *Alice* itself —*Aunt Judy's Magazine* which belonged to Juliana Ewing's mother, Mrs. Gatty, shows excellent examples) ; and Dodgson finally sent Tenniel a photograph of one of his child friends, Mary Hilton Badcock, who was the right sort of little girl for the pictures. He also told Tenniel that he ought to go and see Miss Badcock and draw her, or at least use a live " model " ; but Tenniel was annoyed at being told how to do his own job, and replied indignantly that he no more needed a model to make pictures for *Alice* than Dodgson needed a copy of the multiplication tables to work out a problem ! He did finally go and visit Mary, however, and made a number of drawings of her ; but he was still annoyed with Dodgson, and advised him to find another artist for *Through the Looking Glass*, and suggested Dicky Doyle (who was the illustrator of Ruskin's *The King of the Golden River* and Dickens' *The Cricket on the Hearth*, besides being the artist who designed the cover of *Punch* which is still in use).

Dodgson wrote to Doyle, but could not persuade him to undertake the job ; and as everyone insisted that Tenniel was *the* ideal illustrator, he approached him once more and at length won his agreement, Tenniel unbending so far as to visit Mary Badcock again—for the drawings in *Through the Looking Glass* show her as a year or so older, and were said at the time to be much better likenesses than any in *Wonderland*.

Dodgson was still most particular about every detail, writing such criticisms as "Don't give Alice so much crinoline," or "The White Knight must not have whiskers ; he must not be made to look old "; but Tenniel also was allowed to make suggestions and criticisms, as for example when he wrote on June 1, 1870 :

"My Dear Dodgson,

I think that when the *jump* occurs in the Railway scene you might very well make Alice lay hold of the Goat's *beard* as being the object nearest to her hand—instead of the old lady's hairs—the jerk would naturally throw them together. Don't think me brutal, but I am bound to say that the 'wasp' chapter doesn't interest me in the least, and I can't see my way to a picture. If you want to shorten the book, I can't help thinking—with all submission—that there is your opportunity . . ." while he wrote again : "A *wasp* in a *wig* is altogether beyond the appliances of art !"—and the "wasp" chapter *was* left out (how one wonders what it was about, and how one envies Tenniel who was perhaps the only person who ever read it !)—which is perhaps why Alice takes such a very short time in getting all the way to the Fourth Square, though to be sure a pawn can jump over a whole square in its first move.

Dodgson was very proud of the Chess frame-work of the story and the "Chess problem" included in the beginning of the book which, he says, "is correctly worked out, so far as the moves are concerned . . . the 'check' of the White King at move 6 [The Lion and the Unicorn], the capture of the Red Knight at move 7 [in his battle with the White Knight], and the final 'check-mate' of the Red King, will be found, by anyone who will take the trouble to set the pieces and play the moves as directed to be strictly in accordance with the laws of the game." Chess experts, however, refuse to agree with Dodgson, and point out many false or impossible moves in the "Game"—an odd fact certainly for a good Chess-player and so careful and exact a scholar as Mr. Dodgson!

As in the earlier book, so here also, he used, besides his recollections of old stories told to the Liddells and perhaps other children, a number of poems which he had written at various earlier dates. The most interesting one is "Jabberwocky," of which the first verse was written at Croft in 1855 and copied into the family magazine *Misch-Masch*; and the rest somewhat later when, during a visit to his cousins the Misses Wilcox, at Whitburn, near Sunderland, the whole party sat down one evening to a game of verse-making, and "Jabberwocky" was produced as Dodgson's contribution.

STANZA   OF   ANGLO - SAXON   POETRY.

```
TWAS  BRYLLYG ,  AND  Yᵉ  SLYTHY  TOVES
DID  GYRE  AND  GYMBLE  IN  Yᵉ  WABE :
ALL  MIMSY  WERE  Yᵉ  BOROGOVES ;
AND  Yᵉ  MOME  RATHS  OUTGRABE .
```

This curious fragment reads thus in modern characters

TWAS BRYLLYG, AND THE SLYTHY TOVES
DID GYRE AND GYMBLE IN, THE WABE'
ALL MIMSY WERE THE BOROGOVES;
AND THE MOME RATHS OUTGRABE.

The meanings of the words are as follows:

BRYLLYG. (derived from the verb to BRYL or BROIL.) "the time of broiling dinner, i.e. the close of the afternoon"

SLYTHY. (compounded of SLIMY and LITHE). "smooth and active

TOVE. a species of Badger. They had smooth white hair, long

72

hind legs. and short horns like a stag. lived chiefly on cheese

GYRE verb (derived from GYAOUR or GIAOUR, "a dog.") "to scratch like a dog"

GYMBLE (whence GIMBLET) to screw out holes in anything

WABE (derived from the verb to SWAB or SOAK) "the side of hill" (from its being soaked by the rain)

MIMSY (whence MIMSERABLE and MISERABLE) "unhappy"

BOROGOVE An extinct kind of Parrot The had no wings beaks turned up, and made their nests under sun-dials lived on veal

MOME (hence SOLEMOME SOLEMONE and SOLEMN) grave

RATH A species of land turtle Head erect mouth like a shark the front fore legs curved out so that the animal walked on it's knees smooth green body lived on swallows and oysters

OUTGRABE past tense of the verb to OUTGRIBE. (it is connected with the old verb to GRIKE or SHRIKE, from which are derived "shriek" and "creak.") "squeaked"

Hence the literal English of the passage is.
"It was evening, and the smooth active badgers were scratching and boring holes in the hill side. all unhappy were the parrots, and the grave turtles squeaked out"

There were probably sun-dials on the top of the hill, and the "borogoves" were afraid that their nests would be undermined The hill was probably full of the nests of "raths", which ran out squeaking with fear on hearing the "toves" scratching outside. This is an obscure, but yet deeply affecting, relic of ancient Poetry

Croft 1855 &c

The verse in *Misch-Masch* is called " Stanza of Anglo-Saxon Poetry," and is unchanged, except that to make it more " olde," " bryllyg, slythy and gymble " are spelt with " y's " instead of " i's " ; it is followed by a very " serious " discourse on the meaning of the verse and the origin of the strange words, agreeing in most respects with Humpty-Dumpty's explanation, but giving many more strange facts than he does, and differing in a few cases. For example:

73

"TOVE. A species of Badger. They had smooth white hair, long hind legs, and short horns like a stag : lived chiefly on cheese . . ."

"GYRE, verb (derived from GYAOUR or GIAOUR, 'a dog'). 'To scratch like a dog' . . ."

"WABE (derived from the verb to SWAB or SOAK). "The side of a hill (from its being soaked by the rain) . . ." [But Humpty-Dumpty's explanation is far better !]

"BOROGOVE. An extinct kind of Parrot. They had no wings, beaks turned up, and made their nests under sun-dials : lived on veal . . ."

"RATH. A species of land turtle. Head erect : mouth like a shark : the fore legs curved out so that the animal walked on its knees : smooth green body : lived on swallows and oysters . . ."

"Hence the literal English of the passage is : ' It was evening, and the smooth active badgers were scratching and boring holes in the hill-side : all unhappy were the parrots ; and the grave turtles squeaked out.' There were probably sundials on the top of the hill, and the ' borogoves ' were afraid that their nests would be undermined. The hill was probably full of the nests of ' raths,' which ran out, squeaking with fear, on hearing the ' toves ' scratching outside. This is an obscure, but yet deeply affecting relic of ancient Poetry."

Of the " portmanteau " words in the rest of the poem, Dodgson explained " frumious " carefully as a key to the others made in the same way : " Take the two words ' fuming ' and ' furious .' Make up your mind that you will say both words, but leave it unsettled which you will say first . . . if you have that rarest of gifts, a perfectly balanced mind, you will say ' frumious '."

A few years after the book was published a little girl asked Dodgson to tell her what some other words meant in " Jabberwocky," and he replied in a letter : " I'm afraid

74

I can't explain ' vorpal blade ' for you—nor yet ' tulgey wood '; but I did make an explanation once for ' uffish thought '—It seems to suggest a state of mind when the voice is gruffish, the manner roughish, and the temper huffish. Then again, as to ' burble ' : if you take the three verbs ' *b*leat,' ' m*ur*mur ' and ' war*ble*,' and select the bits I have underlined, it certainly *makes* ' burble ' : though I am afraid I can't distinctly remember having made it in that way."

The name " Jabberwock " he later described as being made from the real Anglo-Saxon word " wocer " meaning " offspring," and the ordinary word " jabber "—but this was done to suit a magazine issued by an American girls' school and called *The Jabberwock*—i.e., " The result of much excited discussion," and it is not likely that he had this meaning in mind when he first introduced " The Jabberwock with eyes of flame." The Jub-jub bird is not explained— nor yet the " frumious Bandersnatch," though one is tempted to think that he may have known that " Bandar " is Hindustani for a monkey. In later years Dodgson was a devoted reader of Kipling, and bought all his books as soon as they appeared, being particularly fond of *The Jungle Book* (did he ever think how aptly Bagheera or Kaa might have been described as a " Bandar-snatch " ? !). Kipling knew Alice almost by heart, and indeed it seems likely that *Alice* was in everyone's mouth when Kipling was at school (1878-1882)—certainly if we trust *Stalky and Co.* as reliable evidence, for therein " burble," " galumphing," " beamish," " frabjous " and " chortle " are used as if they were perfectly ordinary English words—as indeed they are by now, to- gether with " whiffling." And it would be a very good thing if " brillig " were also added to the language, as a name for that awkward part of the day between tea and dinner which is really neither afternoon nor evening !

Things Anglo-Saxon play quite a large part in *Through the*

Looking Glass, for besides " Jabberwocky " we have the Hatter and the Hare from *Wonderland* translated into Anglo-Saxon Messengers as " Hatta " and " Haigha," dressed in Anglo-Saxon costumes (except for Hatta's hat !) and going into " Anglo-Saxon Attitudes " on every opportunity. Both the costumes and the attitudes are genuinely Anglo-Saxon, and may be found in the " Caedmon Manuscript " which both Dodgson and Tenniel could easily have seen at the Bodleian Library in Oxford.

Hatters were mad long before Wonderland (and hares still behave oddly in March), just as the health of the young ladies in Dodgson's home country had for many years been drunk to the toast of " The Cheshire Cats ! "—(perhaps the term was invented by the ladies in the next shire who were referred to as " The Lancashire Witches ")—but otherwise all the characters in *Wonderland* were invented by Dodgson, and only one incident, the theft of the tarts, is suggested by an old rhyme. But in the country *Through the Looking Glass* dwelt many persons already known from the popular Nursery Rhymes, most of which were first collected and written down when Dodgson was still a boy, by an antiquarian called Halliwell-Phillips. In his collections we find " Tweedle-dum and Tweedle-dee," " The Lion and the Unicorn," the first verse of " The Queen of Hearts," and a version of "Humpty-Dumpty," all nearly as quoted by Dodgson in the *Alice* books. There are other suggestions here too : " I love my love with an A " (" with an H " in *Looking Glass*) ; " Fiddle-de-de ! Fiddle-de-dee ! "—the first line of a set of verses about the fly and the bumble-bee (but whether " Fiddle-de-de " is English or not, Mr. Halliwell-Phillips fails to tell us !) ; " Birds of a feather flock together" (but are flamingoes and mustard both birds, as the Duchess seemed to think ?). It is also stated in the rhyme beginning " Dickery-dickery dare " that " The pig flew up in the air " —so the Walrus and the Carpenter had some reason for discussing " whether pigs have wings " ; and there is " Hush-a-bye baby on the tree top," which becomes " Hush-a-bye lady in Alice's lap."

There is, by the way, another rhyme, quite unknown now, but contained in a very popular children's book of the period, *The Golden Thread*, by Norman MacLeod, published the year before the *Alice* story was told to the Liddell children on their river picnic, where a squirrel sings :

" And I waken up the bat,
Who flies off with a scream,
For he thinks that I'm the cat
Pouncing on him in his dream "—

which, in dreams at least, seems to answer Alice's question : " Do cats eat bats ? "

Very few of the poems in *Through the Looking-Glass* are actual parodies in the way that most of those in Wonderland are : there is " To the Looking-Glass world it was Alice that said," which is mis-taken directly from Scott's " Bonnie Dundee " ; there is " Hush-a-bye lady in Alice's lap "— and that is almost all. " The Walrus and the Carpenter " is written in the metre of a serious poem by Thomas Hood called " Eugene Aram," yet it is not really a parody of it ; but " The Aged, Aged Man " might be called a parody of a longish poem by Wordsworth, " Resolution and Independence, or The Leech-Gatherer," but it is the spirit of the poem that is burlesqued, rather than the actual wording, and such a verse as the following is the nearest approach to direct parody in the whole poem :

" A gentle answer did the old man make,
In courteous speech which forth he slowly drew :
And him with further words I thus bespake,
' What occupation do you here pursue ?
This is a lonesome place for one like you.'
Ere he replied, a flash of mild surprise
Broke from the sable orbs of his yet vivid eyes."

And that, as the White Knight might have said, is what the poem really *is*; but the *tune*, as Alice realised, was not his own invention : it is that of a little song by Thomas Moore which begins :

> " I give thee all—I can no more—
> Tho' poor the off'ring be ;
> My heart and lute are all the store
> That I can bring to thee."

" The Aged, Aged Man " was not written specially for *Through the Looking Glass*, indeed an earlier version of it was published in *The Train* for October, 1856, and was merely polished up and improved to go in the book. It is too long to quote here in full, but two verses will show the kind of alterations that were made in it :

> " But I was thinking of a way
> To multiply by ten,
> And always, in the answer, get
> The question back again.
> I did not hear a word he said,
> But kicked that old man calm,
> And said ' Come tell me how you live ! '
> And pinched him in the arm.
>
> . . . .
>
> ' I sometimes dig for buttered rolls,
> Or set limed twigs for crabs ;
> I sometimes search the flowery knolls
> For wheels of hansom cabs.
> And that's the way (he gave a wink)
> I get my living here,
> And very gladly will I drink
> Your Honour's health in beer.' "

It was said by some people that the White Knight was suggested by a comic knight called Hudibras who is the hero of the long poem by Samuel Butler written in the middle of the seventeenth century. This character carried his rations in his boots as he rode about, and rats and mice came to eat his supplies, and were trapped by Hudibras who would catch them under the hammer of his pistols ; and when he mounted his horse he did it so vigorously :

> " That he had almost tumbled over
> With his own weight, but did recover,
> By laying hold on tail and mane
> Which oft he used instead of rein."

But when this was suggested to Dodgson, he wrote : " I have certainly no consciousness of having borrowed the idea of the inventions of the White Knight from anything in Hudibras. . . The character of the White Knight was meant to suit the speaker in the poem (i.e., " The Aged, Aged Man "). . . "

A poem which he *had* read, however, and which influenced " The Garden of Live Flowers," was Tennyson's great " monodrama," *Maud*, where (in the section, number XXII, beginning : " Come into the garden, Maud ") you will find all the flowers mentioned by Dodgson, except the Tiger-Lily. When he wrote the story, he had a Passion-flower instead, as in *Maud*, but he changed it to the Tiger-Lily when it was pointed out to him that the name " Passion-flower " had a religious association. But such a verse as this is really very like the moment when the Flowers hear the Red Queen's footsteps :

> " There has fallen a splendid tear
> From the passion-flower at the gate.
> She is coming, my dove, my dear ;
> She is coming, my life, my fate ;
> The red rose cries, ' She is near, she is near ' ;
> And the white rose weeps, ' She is late ' ;
> The larkspur listens, ' I hear, I hear ' ;
> And the lily whispers, ' I wait ' . . ."

79

At first Dodgson thought of calling his new book *Looking-Glass House, and what Alice saw there*, and even had a title-page and a few leaves printed in 1870, just to see what it would look like. But his friend Canon Liddon of Christ Church suggested *Through the Looking-Glass, and What Alice Found There*, which is still the correct title of the book,

In 1871, when the new story was about to appear. Dodgson suddenly felt that the picture of the Jabberwock might be too frightening for small children—certainly if he used it as a frontispiece, as he had intended ; and so he had a letter printed and sent round, with a copy of the picture, to the mothers of a number of his child-friends : " I should be grateful to have your opinion, tested by exhibiting the picture to any children you think fit . . ." but he decided finally to keep the picture, though not as the frontispiece, which place of honor was given to the White Knight; and worthily so, for surely he is one of the most delightful characters in either of the books.

Indeed the characters in the *Alice* books are more intimately known to us than those in almost any other works of fiction, and have become a part of our language ; and it shows the surprising genius of Charles Dodgson that chess-men, playing cards, a group of animals and some characters out of nursery-rhymes already well known, are all inevitably and unmistakably his own creations, made by him once and for all.

But however well known they may be to us, it is still most interesting to see how he himself pictured them, and how he described one or two of them some years later when the books were being made into a play. Alice, he describes as " loving, first—loving and gentle . . . then courteous—courteous to *all*, high or low, grand or grotesque, King or Caterpillar, even as though she were herself a King's daughter, and her clothing of wrought gold : then trustful, ready to accept the wildest impossibilities with all that utter

trust that only dreamers know; and lastly, curious—
wildly curious, and with the eager enjoyment of Life that
comes only in the happy hours of childhood. . .

"And the White Rabbit, what of *him* ? . . . a contrast,
distinctly. For *her* 'youth,' 'audacity,' 'vigour,' and
'swift directness of purpose,' read 'elderly,' 'timid,'
'feeble,' and 'nervously shilly-shallying,' and you will
get something of what I meant him to be. I *think* the White
Rabbit should wear spectacles. I am sure his voice should
quaver, and his knees quiver, and his whole air suggest
a total inability to say 'Bo' to a goose !

". . . It was certainly hard on my Muse to expect her to
sing of *Three* Queens, within such brief compass, and yet
to give each her own individuality. Each, of course, had to
preserve, through all her eccentricities, a certain queenly
dignity. *That* was essential. And for distinguishing traits,
I pictured to myself the Queen of Hearts as a sort of embodi-
ment of ungovernable passion—a blind and aimless Fury.
The Red Queen I pictured as a Fury, but of another type ;
her passion must be cold and calm ; she must be formal and
strict, yet not unkindly ; pedantic to the tenth degree, the
concentrated essence of all governesses ! Lastly the White
Queen seemed, to my dreaming fancy, gentle, stupid, fat and
pale ; helpless as an infant ; and with a slow, maundering,
bewildered air about her just *suggesting* imbecility, but never
quite passing into it. . ."

Through the Looking-Glass was published in December,
1871 (though it was dated 1872), and no unexpected fate
befell the first edition, in which the pictures were printed
quite well enough this time to satisfy both Dodgson and
Tenniel. Although the Looking-Glass world was suggested
by Alice Raikes, and the pictures made from Mary Badcock,
the heroine was still really Alice Liddell ; and not only
does the poem at the beginning refer again to " The pleasance of our fairy-tale," but the one which ends it, perhaps

the best serious poem that Dodgson ever wrote, besides telling of :

> " A boat, beneath a sunny sky
> Lingering onward dreamily
> In an evening of July—
> Children three that nestle near,
> Eager eye and willing ear. . ."

also gives the full name " Alice Pleasance Liddell " as an acrostic. (The first letters of the lines just quoted giving " ALICE," and so on with the rest.)

And this time there were no bad reviews : *Through the Looking-Glass* took its place at once beside *Wonderland*, making with it almost, if not quite, the best known, best loved book in the English language—*Alice*.

After which one must, in all fairness, quote the remark of a child whom Dodgson asked if she had read the books : " Oh yes, I've read both of them, and I think . . . I think *Through the Looking-Glass* is more stupid than *Alice's Adventures in Wonderland*. Don't *you* think so ? "

CHAPTER VI

MR. DODGSON OF CHRIST CHURCH

IT is surprising how little difference the fame of " Lewis Carroll " and his works made to the Rev. C. L. Dodgson living his quiet, methodical life at Christ Church, lecturing to his mathematical pupils, entertaining his child-friends, working out puzzles in logic or mathematics—though now thinking rather more seriously of what he was to write about next over his famous pen-name. But he did not neglect his University work, and serious books still appeared by " C. L. Dodgson " : text-books for students, difficult treatises on higher mathematics, problems in logic—though most of these would have been forgotten long ago had they not been written by the author of *Alice*. The titles of some of them will show what kind of books they were, and that is almost as much as anyone will want to know about them now—for few people would be interested to read *A Guide to the Mathematical Student*, or *The Condensation of Determinants*, any more than *Algebraical Formulae for Responsions* and *Curiosa Mathematica*.

There is a story, still often quoted as a fact, that Queen Victoria, having read *Alice* with great delight, commanded the author to send her copies of all his other books (or to dedicate his next book to her)—and was definitely " not amused " by the parcel of mathematical books which she received. This is only a legend, and Dodgson himself was so annoyed by it that at length he declared in print that " it is utterly false in every particular : nothing even resembling it has ever occurred." But it is just the sort of mistake which might have occurred among readers less important than Her Majesty.

For there were dozens of people at Oxford, even attending Dodgson's lectures, who never dreamt that this rather dull and ordinary don with the trying stammer was the great Lewis Carroll, just as there were thousands of people all the world over who were enthusiastic admirers of Lewis Carroll, but had never heard of C. L. Dodgson.

"WHAT I LOOK LIKE WHEN I'M LECTURING"
A drawing by Lewis Carroll

Yet he was very much one and same person, and even if his lectures were dull, he found it difficult to keep his sense of fun out of almost everything else that he did and wrote and talked about.

Later in life he became something of a hermit and disliked

to be disturbed, but he always took an interest in the affairs of the University, attending " Congregation " (as the weekly meetings open to all Senior Members are called) occasionally, if not regularly, where he spoke from time to time on subjects that interested him—the appointment of the Professor of Philology, for example ; or whether women should be admitted to the University examinations. And on one occasion, at least, he was unable to restrain his sense of the humor of words, for when one speaker declared with much eloquence that the chief duty of the University was to turn out as many good professors as possible, Dodgson rose slowly and remarked: "Quite right! Quite right! Turn them out! Turn them out!"

He took a serious interest in these matters, however, even if he expressed his interest in a humorous way. Often when there was some question which was being much discussed (and at that time Oxford people took such things more seriously than now, probably because there were fewer distractions in those days of unmarried Fellows and Tutors !) Dodgson would make his contribution in the form of a little pamphlet. Sometimes these were serious productions, when they usually bore the author's name, " Charles L. Dodgson," or even in later years " Lewis Carroll," when the question was of interest outside Oxford and the more famous name would carry greater weight : *Natural Science at Oxford*, *Parliamentary Representation*, *Some Popular Fallacies about Vivisection* and *Resident Women Students*, are the names of some of these serious pamphlets.

But often also his contribution would be in humorous form ; and although these little works are concerned with people and events of no interest whatsoever to us now, and in spite of the fact that their author intended them to be the works of C. L. Dodgson of Oxford (or " D.C.L." as most of them are signed) and not the more widely known Lewis Carroll, some at least still make pleasant reading. Of the best of these the first is too complicated to quote in part; but the second, *The Dynamics of a Parti-cle*, which is a skit on a particular election of Oxford candidates to Parliament in 1865, is a delight from start to finish. It pretends to be a serious mathematical treatise, but is in reality a series of jokes, very much in the " Lewis Carroll " style, and anyone with even the slightest knowledge of Geometry can appreciate the humor of such definitions as:

"PLAIN SUPERFICIALITY is the character of a speech, in which any two points being taken, the speaker is found to lie wholly with regard to those two points.

" PLAIN ANGER is the inclination of two voters to one another, who meet together, but whose views are not in the same direction.

" Let it be granted that a speaker may digress from any one point to any other point. . .

" PROPOSITIONS. . . To find the value of a given Examiner. *Example*—A takes in ten books in the Final Examination, and gets a Third Class; B takes in the Examiners, and gets a Second. Find the value of the Examiners in terms of books. Find also their value in terms in which no examination is held. . . "

Another pamphlet deals with an offer to supply the University with new rooms for experiments in the Physical Sciences; Dodgson considered that the scientists wanted far too many rooms and that their reasons for needing them were not good enough, so he parodied their request with one of his own for new accommodation to carry out mathematical experiments, for which, amongst other things, he declared that there were needed:

" A very large room for calculating Greatest Common Measure. To this a small one might be attached for Least Common Multiple. A piece of open ground for keeping Roots and practising their extraction: it would be advisable to keep Square Roots by themselves, as their corners are apt to damage others. . . A large room, which might be darkened, and fitted up with a magic lantern for the purpose of exhibiting Circulating Decimals in the act of circulation. . . A narrow strip of ground . . for . . testing practically whether Parallel Lines meet or not. . . A small photographic room would be desirable, both for general use and for representing the various phenomena of Gravity, Disturbance of Equilibrium, Resolution, etc., which affect the features during severe mathematical operations. . ."

" A thing of beauty is a joy for ever."

East view of the new Belfry, Ch. Ch., as seen from the Meadow

FRONTISPIECE FROM *THE NEW BELFRY*

By far the most amusing of all is *The New Belfry at Christ Church*, *Oxford*, written and published in 1872 when the bells had been taken out of the Cathedral tower and put into a square wooden belfry of hideous aspect just over the entrance to the dining hall in the great quadrangle (" Tom Quad ")—much to the horror of most of the inhabitants of Oxford. The wooden box containing the bells was afterwards concealed by the pleasant-looking stone tower which is still to be seen there ; but in 1872 most people feared that the wooden monstrosity would simply be left as it was. The whole of *The New Belfry* makes good reading, and to quote a few "Chapters" will give some idea of Dodgson's excellent sense of burlesque and of quiet, subtle humor:

"*On the etymological significance of the new Belfry*. . . The word "Belfry" is derived from the French *bel*, "beautiful, becoming, meet," and from the German *frei*, "free, unfettered, secure, safe." Thus the word is strictly equivalent to "meat-safe," to which the new belfry bears a resemblance so perfect as almost to amount to coincidence. . .

"*On the style of the new Belfry*. . . The style is that which is usually known as "Early Debased": very early, and remarkably debased. . .

"*On the chief architectural merit of the new Belfry*. . . Its chief merit is its simplicity—a simplicity so pure, so profound, in a word, so *simple*, that no other word will fitly describe it. . .

"*On the other architectural merits of the new Belfry*. . . The Belfry has no other architectural merits. . ."

And so the fun proceeds merrily ; the Belfry is likened to a box, a Greek Lexicon, a bathing-machine, a tea-caddy, a bar of soap, and a clothes-horse; but his favorite name for it is thus explained: "What traveller is there, to whose lips, when first he enters that great educational establishment and gazes on this its newest decoration, the words do not rise unbidden—' Thou tea-chest '. . . "

In another pamphlet, in style a parody of Walton's *Compleat Angler*, Dodgson dealt again with the "Tea-Chest," and also with other architectural changes at Christ Church, "The Tunnel" and "The Trench," the whole being called *The Vision of the Three T's* ; and there were also verse parodies on Oxford questions and about Oxford personalities, such as the delightful "rhymed alphabet" of 1864, part of which runs :

" I am the Author, a rhymer erratic—
  J is for [Jowett], who lectures in Attic:
  K is for [Kitchen], than attic much warmer,
  L is for [Liddell], relentless reformer.

Of these, Jowett was the Professor of Greek (" Attic "
is the ancient Greek dialect used by most of the great
writers) on the subject of whose salary Dodgson wrote the
earliest of his humorous " topical " pamphlets ; Dean
Kitchen was the father of one of Dodgson's favourite
child-friends, Alexandra (always known as Xie) ; and
Liddell, of course, was the Dean of Christ Church and
father of Lorina, Alice and Edith.

In 1874 these humorous pamphlets were collected by
Dodgson into one volume called *Notes by an Oxford Chiel*.

Although Dodgson seems to have found it hard to form
any really close friendships with people of his own age, he
was well liked by many of his fellow students at Christ
Church (besides a stray outsider from another college, such
as Canon Duckworth), and there were certainly two who
might be described at least as intimate acquaintances—
his old school-friend Thomas Vere Baynes, and Canon
Henry Liddon. Dodgson and Liddon were at Christ
Church together for nearly their whole lives, and although
they never got beyond calling each other by their surnames,
seem to have appreciated one another's company in a sincere
if rather formal way. Certainly during the Long Vacation
of 1867 these two went for a tour through Germany and
Poland to Russia, and home by way of France. This was
Dodgson's only foreign tour, and he recorded it very carefully in his diary, both amusing details and serious
impressions.

This, for example, is how he described the way in which
the Germans decorated their cities : " The two principles
of Berlin architecture appear to me to be these : On the
house tops, wherever there is a convenient place, put up the

figure of a man ; he is best placed standing on one leg. Wherever there is room on the ground, put either a circular group of busts on pedestals, in consultation, all looking inwards—or else the colossal figure of a man killing, about to kill, or having killed (the present tense is preferred) a beast ; the more pricks the beast has, the better—in fact a dragon is the correct thing, but if that is beyond the artist, he may content himself with a lion or a pig. The beast-killing principle has been carried out everywhere with a relentless monotony, which makes some parts of Berlin look like a fossil slaughter-house." Here also he met " a very pleasant German gentleman . . . who was most good-natured in guessing at my meaning, and helping me out with my sentences of what would have been very bad German, if it had deserved the name of German at all."

In Russia the language problem was even more of a difficulty, and though they had many introductions to eminent people, most of whom could talk English or French, some amusing situations cropped up from time to time. There was the case of the cab-driver who tried to cheat Dodgson over the fare—but Dodgson could at least count in Russian, and when the driver had indignantly refused the correct fare of thirty *kopecks*, demanding forty, Dodgson quietly took it back and would not again offer him more than twenty-five.

On another occasion Canon Liddon had left his overcoat in the hotel cloakroom, and as Dodgson's little Russian phrase-book did not contain the word " coat," they had some difficulty in retrieving it from the waiting-maid. " Liddon began by exhibiting his coat [i.e., his jacket], with much gesticulation, including the taking it half-off. To our delight, she appeared to understand at once—left the room, and returned in a minute with—a large clothes-brush. On this Liddon tried a further and more energetic demonstration ; he took off his coat, and laid it at her feet, pointed downwards (to intimate that in the lower regions was the object of his desire), smiled with an expression of the joy and gratitude with which he would receive it, and put the coat on again. Once more a gleam of intelligence lighted up the plain but expressive features of the young person; she was absent much longer this time, and when she returned, she brought, to our dismay, a large cushion and a pillow, and began to prepare the sofa for the nap that she now saw clearly was the thing the dumb gentleman wanted. A happy thought occurred to me, and I hastily drew a sketch representing Liddon, with one coat on,

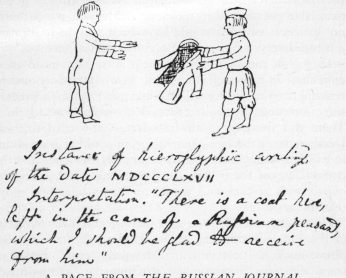

Instance of hieroglyphic writing
of the date MDCCCLXVII
Interpretation. "There is a coat here,
left in the care of a Russian peasant,
which I should be glad to receive
from him"

A PAGE FROM *THE RUSSIAN JOURNAL*

receiving a second and larger one from the hands of a benignant Russian peasant. . ."

Wherever they went in Germany, Poland and Russia, Dodgson and Liddon visited churches and attended the various services. Liddon's fame as a preacher was known

91

even in Russia, where high Church dignitaries made them welcome, and even persuaded him to preach in their churches. Dodgson was interested in the various forms of religious service, too ; but he went to theatres alone— in Germany, Russia and France, and records at least one child actress, " one of the cleverest children I ever saw, who could not have been more than six years old," but he does not seem to have made any foreign child friends, and was not attracted by " the Russian children, whose type of face is ugly as a rule, and plain as an exception."

Besides his interest in the services, Dodgson was an enthusiastic admirer of good Church architecture ; and was particularly impressed by Cologne cathedral, " which I will not attempt to describe further than by saying it was the most beautiful of all churches I have ever seen, or can imagine. If one could imagine the spirit of devotion embodied in any material form, it would be in such a building." And Liddon records in *his* diary that " Dodgson was overcome by the beauty of Cologne Cathedral. I found him leaning against the rails of the Choir, and sobbing like a child. When the verger came to show us over the chapels, he got out of the way. He said that he could not bear the harsh voice of the man in the presence of so much beauty."

In his own diary Dodgson was more ready to dwell on the amusing side of their experiences, and the tour concludes with an account of their visit to the Paris Exhibition, during which, besides other delights, they " passed a pavilion where Chinese music was going on, and paid half a franc to go in and listen to it nearer : and certainly the difference between being inside and outside was worth the half-franc—only the outside was the pleasanter of the two. It was just the kind of music which, once heard, one desires never to hear again. . ."

Although Dodgson seems to have enjoyed his tour with

Liddon, the experiment was never repeated, and never again did he go much further from Oxford than his usual summer resort of Eastbourne and his winter visits to his sisters at Guildford.

For in 1868 Dodgson's father had died, and so the visits to Croft came to an end, and the family was broken up and scattered. Dodgson's brothers were already following their various callings in different parts of the world, and the unmarried sisters left the big rectory and settled in a small house at Guildford, which henceforth became all that Dodgson ever had of a home in the truer, more intimate sense. He felt the loss of his father very acutely, for there had never been any shadow over the trust and affection which always existed between them, and described it long afterwards in a letter written to a friend who had just suffered a similar loss : " The greatest blow that has ever fallen on *my* life was the death, nearly thirty years ago, of my own dear father . . . " ; but nevertheless found that his own absolute faith in the reality of the life to come made " such a parting holy and beautiful, instead of being merely a blank despair."

Dodgson by this time was nearing middle age, and for some years he had been well settled into his life at Oxford. His shyness, though he did not allow it to be any hindrance to his work, and although it did not prevent him from being on good terms with the senior members of at least his own college, still kept him very much to himself, though he would pay occasional calls on the parents of his child-friends : and though, as he grew older, he found himself less ill at ease in the company of young women—whom he could regard more and more as children rather than as his own contemporaries. Also the realisation of his growing fame as an author and recognition in the University as a valuable senior member (though he was never very success-ful as a lecturer !) made him less diffident and more sure of himself. But for all that, as he grew older he became more of a recluse, more regular and methodical in his habits, less and less inclined to vary the usual routine of every day.

At Oxford his life was simple in the extreme, and another member of the Christ Church Senior Common Room, Professor York Powell, who knew him as well as most of his associates, says that " he rose early, worked nearly all day standing at his desk, with the barest apology for lunch ; and a brief smart walk now and then in the afternoon, or a call at some friend's house, were his only diversion. Hall-dinner and a chat with a friend in his own room afterward, with some more work after, till he went to bed. He rarely dined out, and only occasionally invited particular friends to dine with him. He wanted all his time for his work, he said, and he often told us he found his days too short. He had very good health, and was seldom out of sorts for a day. . . "

In this way passed most of Dodgson's life at Oxford, particularly in term time, which was when York Powell had most opportunity to observe him. During the vacation he was not quite so strict with himself, and was then able to spend more time with children, often inviting them to accompany him on his walks—which were not at all what we should understand by short ! Four or five miles was the usual distance of a Dodgson " constitutional," and his favourite routes were by way of " Mesopotamia "—the long, winding strip of land shaded by tall trees which lies between two levels of the river Cherwell—and thence up to the top of Headington Hill, all woodland and open fields at that time ; or along another country road to the little village of Iffley with its lovely old Norman church, across the Thames by the weir and lock, and back to Oxford along the tow-path and across Folly Bridge ; or " the four-mile grind " along the tow-path beyond Iffley to Kennington, and then back again by the road below Bagley Wood.

But once at least he invited Ethel Arnold on an afternoon expedition which was to end by the two of them walking back from Woodstock—about twelve miles between lunch and dinner—and was mildly surprised when Ethel regretted that she could not accompany him that afternoon!

Returned from his walk shortly before 7 p.m., Dodgson would proceed, clad in his long black gown as befitted a Master of the "House," to dinner in the great, shadowy Hall where the candles in their silver candlesticks glimmered on the long lines of portraits above the dark panelling on either side, on the silver mugs and cruets, the white napery and the tall sugar-sifters. On the raised platform at the upper end, at "High Table," the "Students" and Professors, Tutors and Lecturers dined together, with the Undergraduates below them at the long tables by the great open fires where the logs blazed in huge iron fire-baskets. And when dinner was ended the "Dons" would all depart through the little door in the panelling behind "High Table" and down to the Senior Common Room to sit round the polished tables for dessert, and to drink the old College port and other wines, and talk for as long into the evening as they wished.

Dodgson was a constant member of "Common Room," living always in College, and dined there most nights in the week (and "out of term" the Senior members dine in Common Room); and in 1882 he accepted the post of Curator, which he held for nearly ten years. This office is held by some reliable Fellow in each college, and generally is not a very wearing job. But Dodgson found the organisation at Christ Church in a very bad state, and with his usual thoroughness and care for detail, he set to work on his new duties. These included the accounts of Common Room expenditure, making arrangements to have the room decorated, ordering wines, dealing with the servants, seeing to the comfort of the cat, ordering newspapers and magazines, instituting afternoon tea in 1884, and writing as many as eight hundred letters a year on college business. The sort of letter he was called upon to write is shown by one sent to Arthur Girdlestone in October 1889: ". . . You have indeed a curious idea of that ancient Club, the Christ Church Common Room, to suppose it to consist of *resident* members only! We have about 40 resident members, who pay, as you know, 10s. 6d. a Quarter, and about 400 *non*-resident members, who pay, as you *don't* know, 1s. a Quarter. . ."

After a year as Curator, Dodgson wished to resign, as he found that his duties were seriously interfering with his literary work, leaving him even less time than when he was a Lecturer; but his colleagues all desired him to continue in office, and thinking it his duty to do so, he retained it for another eight years, not without some mild protests from time to time. These were usually made in form of privately printed pamphlets—*Twelve Months in a Curatorship, Three Years in a Curatorship*, and so on—where his humor often got the better of his serious attempts to describe what duties he had performed during his period of office; he invented rules for the Curator and the Committee—"if the Curator shall complain of cold, it shall be the duty of the Committee to make things warm for him"; he listed the many things not done during the year, including the repairing of an electric bell which "was destroyed by Mr. S. Owen," and which Mr. Baynes had offered to have put in order—"nine years have elapsed since this record was made, but the kind feeling, which prompted the offer of Mr. Baynes, is as strong as ever . . ."; and on finding that as well as Curator he was officially a member of the Committee, whose duty is to help the Curator, deduced that it was therefore his duty to help himself—but " I decline to say whether this clause has ever brightened existence for me—or whether, in the shades of evening, I may ever have been observed leaving the C.R. cellars with a small but suspicious-looking bundle . . ."

Although he became so much of a recluse towards the end of his life, and even made a habit of refusing all invitations to dinner (though he would " drop in " on particular friends uninvited) Dodgson for his first twenty or thirty years at Oxford was not at all averse to meeting people—particularly famous people.

His favourite hobby was photography—and a hundred years ago this was far from being the easy business that it now is. All photographs had to be " time-exposures " ; the camera was a large and unwieldy instrument mounted on a heavy tripod ; the photograph was taken on to a glass plate coated with chemicals, and the photographer had to develop this himself, in a " dark room " lit only by a red lamp (an oil lamp in those days), which was also most complicated.

Dodgson's humorous poem " Hiawatha's Photographing," which appeared first in *The Train* for December, 1857, gives us some idea of the method in a form sufficiently amusing to quote—particularly as, when the poem was reprinted in *Phantasmagoria* in 1869, most of the " scientific details " were omitted .

> " From his shoulder Hiawatha
> Took the camera of rosewood—
> Made of sliding, folding rosewood—
> Neatly put it all together.
> In its case it lay compactly,
> Folded into nearly nothing ;
> But he opened out its hinges,
> Pushed and joined the joints and hinges
> Till it looked all squares and oblongs,
> Like a complicated figure
> In the second book of Euclid.

'This he perched upon a tripod,
And the family, in order
Sat before him for their pictures—
Mystic, awful was the process.

    First, a piece of glass he coated
With collodion, and plunged it
In a bath of lunar caustic
Carefully dissolved in water—
There he left it certain minutes.

    Secondly, my Hiawatha
Made with cunning hand a mixture
Of the acid pyro-gallic,
And of glacial-acetic,
And of alcohol and water—
This developed all the picture.

    Finally he fixed each picture
With a saturate solution
Which was made of hyposulphite,
Which, again, was made of soda. . . "

Yet in spite of all the difficulties of early photography, Dodgson produced some of the very best photographs taken during the Victorian period—and it is constantly a surprise, when reading lives of the famous men and women of the time, to find again and again " Photograph by Lewis Carroll " beneath the best portraits in the book.

In the late 'fifties and early 'sixties, Dodgson was well acquainted with the Rossetti family—particularly Dante Gabriel the artist and poet, and his sister the poetess Christina—and took a number of photographs of them, singly and in groups, and those which have survived are among the very best likenesses of this fascinating family. Dodgson visited Rossetti fairly frequently at the time when he was writing *Alice in Wonderland*, and the strange selection of pets kept by the poet-artist in his big, shady garden, vividly recall the creatures who took part in the Caucus

Race. Christina Rossetti says that "there were some of them at liberty. I particularly recall Bobby, a little owl with a very large face and a beak of a sort of eggshell green; a woodchuck, a deer, and a wombat... With such inhabitants Tudor House and its grounds became a sort of Wonder-

THE ROSSETTI FAMILY
Photograph by Lewis Carroll

land; and once the author of *Wonderland* photographed us in the garden..." Gabriel's wombat, a furry, sleepy little creature, was said by another artist friend, Ford Madox Brown, to have been the original of the Dormouse in *Alice*.

Dodgson was always interested in art, and besides his early illustrations to the family magazines, and to *Alice's Adventures Underground*, he was in the habit until the end of his life of trying to sketch children on the sea-shore, and in the studio of at least one friend where he would spend long hours, even as late as 1896. "He confessed to having no interest in boy or grown-up female models," she records, "having the 'bad taste' to find more beauty in the undeveloped than the mature form. . . I cannot say his drawings were very good, in spite of his concentration and enthusiasm. . . " But he admired the art of others, particularly that of Sir Noel Paton, Arthur Hughes, and Gertrude Thompson, by all of whom he had pictures which hung in his rooms at Christ Church. He made a special expedition to London in 1883 to see the exhibition of Rossetti's pictures, his favorite being one of the finest, an unfinished painting called "Found."

Other artist friends included Holman Hunt, and Ruskin (who told Dodgson that he did not show sufficient promise to continue drawing seriously) and he greatly admired the drawings of Kate Greenaway, and of Linley Sambourne (who illustrated *The Water Babies*) besides his own illustrators, Tenniel, with whom he did not get on well, and Henry Holiday who always ranked among his more intimate acquaintances.

Many friendships were started by Dodgson in his earlier years, but few of them lasted for very long—not the Tennysons, the Rossettis, the MacDonalds, Charlotte Yonge, nor any of the artists whom he knew and photographed between about 1860 and 1870—and besides those few of his child-friends who did not drift away from him as they grew up, his longest friendships were those with Liddon, Baynes, and the actress Ellen Terry.

His interest in photography did not continue much after 1870, for as soon as the easy "dry-plate" method came in, he abandoned the amusement. But by then he had taken an enormous number, particularly pictures of children, who were always his favorite subjects.

Dodgson's excellence as a photographer lay in the skill with which he posed his models, the simplicity and naturalness which they show in all his photographs, and the minute care and patience which he spent on arriving as near perfection as possible.

He began with open-air photography, particularly when he wanted to make a large group; the delicious jumble of MacDonald children with himself in the middle (taken with the aid of a string to move the shutter), for example; the Rossetti family in their back garden; and many other groups of croquet players, children, and so on. But very soon he started to take photographs in a little studio which was made for him on the flat leads above his rooms at Christ Church, where all his child-friends for many years experienced the mixed pleasures of posing for him.

"It was no joke," wrote Ethel Arnold, one of his Oxford child-friends, "being photographed in those days; and for a nervous child, dressed up as a Heathen Chinee, a beggar-child, or a fisher-maiden, to keep still for forty-five seconds at a time was no mean ordeal. I was an extremely bad subject. . . !" And another, Evelyn Hatch, recalls that "boys as well as girls were invited to be photographed, but opinions were somewhat divided as to whether it were really a great treat. It meant much patience, for the photographer was always determined to get his picture 'just right,' and it must be owned that there is a certain expression of boredom on the faces of some of his young models, who remember that the studio was very hot, and that they used to get very tired of sitting still."

But most children found it very much worth while being photographed; for the fun of dressing up in the wonderful medley of costumes which Uncle Dodgson kept in the long cupboards in his studio, and of being posed in the oddest attitudes and the most exciting groups—St. George killing the Dragon, for example, or some other unexpected scene. There was also the thrill of watching the plate being developed in the dark-room, of standing on a big box so as to see over the edge of the high table and the sink where Dodgson was dipping his plates into the strange-smelling solutions, and the pictures themselves were slowly becoming visible.

But most of all an afternoon's photography was worth while for the sake of having tea afterwards with Uncle Dodgson in the big room with the corner turrets, and of sitting by the fire listening to his stories.

It is not likely that any of the children ever forgot to come when once they had been invited to be photographed : but Dodgson himself did forget on one occasion at least, when his little friend Annie Rogers, aged about eleven, received the following apology, which her brother (who also remembers being photographed by Dodgson nearly eighty years ago) has allowed me to copy from the carefully hoarded letter which is still treasured, together with a number of the photographs themselves :

" My dear Annie,

This is indeed dreadful. You have no idea of the grief I am in while I write. I am obliged to use an umbrella to keep the tears from running down on to the paper. Did you come yesterday to be photographed ? and were you very angry ? Why was I not there ? Well the fact was this —I went out for a walk with Bibkins, my dear Friend Bibkins —we went many miles from Oxford—fifty—a hundred say. As we were passing a field of sheep a thought crossed my mind, and I said solemnly ' Dobkins, what o'clock is is ? ' ' Three ' said Fizkins, surprised at my manner. Tears ran down my cheeks. ' It is the HOUR ' I said, ' tell me, tell me Hopkins, what day is it ? ' ' Why, Monday, of course,' said Lupkins. ' Then it is the DAY ' I groaned, I wept, I screamed. The sheep crowded round me, and rubbed their affectionate noses against mine. ' Mopkins,' I said, ' you are my oldest friend. Do not deceive me, Nupkins, what year is it ? ' ' Well, I think it's

1867," said Pipkins. " Then it is the YEAR." I screamed so loud that Tapkins fainted. It was all over: I was brought home in a cart, attended by the faithful Wopkins, in several pieces.

When I have recovered a little from the shock, and have been to the sea-side for a few months I will call and arrange another day for photographing. I am too weak to write this for myself, so Zupkins is writing it for me.

Your miserable friend,
LEWIS CARROLL."

CHAPTER VII

SNARKS AND BOOJUMS

HOWEVER much time Mr. Dodgson of Christ Church spent on his mathematics and logical studies, on his University and College duties, in the more social activities of his earlier years and in the entertainment of his continuous series of child-friends, " Lewis Carroll," that now famous author, did not allow his name to be absent for very long from the lists of new books.

When *Alice in Wonderland* was already becoming a household word, and *Through the Looking-Glass* was well on its way to publication, there appeared at the beginning of 1869 a collection of verses called *Phantasmagoria, and Other Poems* intended this time for adult rather than child readers. The " Other Poems " were serious attempts, mostly written during the previous ten or fifteen years, and at the end of his life Dodgson re-issued them separately as *Three Sunsets*— and they are now only to be found in collected editions of his verse. But *Phantasmagoria* and the humorous verses in the first section of the book have been reprinted scores of times, and you may still buy them in the little red miniature edition to match the *Alice* books and *The Hunting of the Snark*.

The long poem, *Phantasmagoria* itself, is clever and amusing—guaranteed to remove all fear of ghosts from the mind of the youngest reader. Yet it is not much more than clever, and would probably be forgotten now if " Lewis Carroll " had written nothing else. Nor are many of the shorter parodies and burlesques really outstanding, good reading though most of them still make : strange, when one considers that most of them must have been written during the years in which Dodgson was also writing "Father William" and "Alice's Evidence," "Jabberwocky" and "The Walrus and the Carpenter"; yet not so strange when we remember how ill at ease Dodgson was with most people of his own age (particularly those who lived and moved in the big world outside the quiet gray walls of the Oxford colleges)—and every bit as much on paper as in person, as the "grown-up" parts of *Sylvie and Bruno* prove in a moment.

However, a few of the verses in the book are almost on the highest level—particularly "Hiawatha's Photographing," "A Sea Dirge," and an acrostic riddle which, besides being amusing in itself, gives us a picture of Dodgson's own personal reactions to the pastime of dancing, always such an absorbing interest at Oxford—particularly during the last century when the three or four great balls held in Commemoration Week at the end of the Summer term were the only dances permitted by the University authorities. After describing the welcome interval for refreshments, the ice-creams ("a tooth-ache in each spoonful!"), the cold chicken, the merry popping of corks, and of how the dance begins anew, Dodgson continues :

" And thus they give the time, that Nature meant
    For peaceful sleep and meditative snores,
To ceaseless din and mindless merriment
    And waste of shoes and floors.

And One (we name him not) that flies the flowers,
    That dreads the dances, and that shuns the salads,
They doom to pass in solitude the hours,
    Writing acrostic-ballads.

How late it grows ! The hour is surely past
    That should have warned us with its double knock?
The twilight wanes, the morning comes at last—
    ' Oh, Uncle, what's o'clock ? '

.   .   .   .

Yet what are all such gaieties to me
Whose thoughts are full of indices and surds?
$$X^2 + 7x + 53$$
$$= \frac{11}{3} \ . \ . \ . \ "$$

It is indeed surprising that Dodgson ever took any of
the friends whom he had known as children to a dance :
far more usual, even to the most pressing invitation, was
such an answer as this :

" As to dancing, my dear, I *never* dance, unless I am
allowed to do it in *my own peculiar way*. There is no use trying to describe it : it has to be seen to be believed. The last
house I tried it in, the floor broke through. But then it was a
poor sort of floor—the beams were only six inches thick,
hardly worth calling beams at all : stone arches are much
more sensible, when dancing, of *my peculiar kind*, is to be
done. Did you ever see the Rhinoceros, and the Hippo-
potamus, at the Zoological Gardens, trying to dance a
minuet together ? It is a touching sight. . . "

On the whole, Dodgson was never particularly social in
the ordinary sense, and later in life he refused all formal
invitations, only " dropping in " on his friends on a day
when he had not been asked. This was largely due to his
dislike of wasting time that could be better spent in work,
and also to a growing fear of people who merely wanted to
meet him because he was a famous author—a " lion," as
celebrities were called in those days. " Thanks for proffer
of luncheon," he wrote to Arthur Girdlestone in 1886,
" but I never go to such things, and, when I do come to
your house, I had rather it should be when there was no
stranger to meet, and especially no ' lion ' . . . I dread
lions. . ." And to Mrs. Hatch, the mother of some of
his favorite Oxford child-friends, who had invited him to
the kind of gathering so common in those days: " Mrs.

Hatch : At Home. Tea 4-6," he replied : "What an awful proposition ! To drink tea from 4 to 6 would tax the constitution even of a hardened tea-drinker. For me, who hardly ever touch it, it would probably be fatal—I must ask you to leave it quite doubtful whether I look in or not—Usually that is the only interval I have between photography and lecture (at 6) . . . "

Another social habit to which he objected was changing into evening dress ; his "morning dress" was always neat in the extreme, the long black coat and trousers of the clergyman, black waistcoat, white bow tie, and black cotton gloves, the whole completed by a top hat whenever he went out, though nothing would ever induce him to wear an overcoat. On the subject of dress he wrote amusingly to one little girl, stating that R.S.V.P. meant "Red Shirt ; Vest Pink," and that doctors had " M.D." after their names so that they could always wear " Morning Dress," even at evening parties, in case they were suddenly sent for—and he suggested that morning dress should be suitable for the evening, as evening dress was so often worn in the morning—that is, at late parties which went on after midnight—or at least that he could qualify as an amateur doctor !

As a matter of fact, Dodgson knew a great deal about medicine and anatomy, and had a very good collection of medical books, which he began to buy so that he should not feel absolutely ignorant and helpless in case of emergency— as he did one day when he saw a man fall down in a fit.

One lure that would always bring Dodgson out of the quiet of his college rooms to partake of the hospitality of some Oxford parent was an invitation from a child or to meet children—a lure that on one occasion produced unexpected results. For one day he was invited to a children's party, and on entering the house and hearing the should get them mixed in your mind. Which would you like best, do you think, a horse that drews you in a cab, or a lady that drews your picture, or a dentist, that drews your teeth, or a Mother, that drews you into her arms, to give you a kiss? And what order would you put the others in? Do you find Looking Glass writing easy to read? I remain, your loving: Lewis Carroll.

Nov. 6, 1893.

My dear Edith,
I was very much
pleased to get your nice
little letter: and I hope
you won't mind letting
Maud have the Nursery
"Alice," now that you have
got the real one. Some
day I will send you the
other book about "Alice," called
"Through the Looking-Glass,"
but you had better have
it just yet, for fear you

FROM LEWIS CARROLL TO EDITH BALL

sound of voices in the drawing-room, he went down on his hands and knees and entered in the character of a bear —only to find that he was in the wrong house, and had come growling in upon a meeting of earnest ladies debating some parish problem, not at all likely to be amused by the sudden appearance of a middle-aged clergyman on all fours— particularly when, on discovering his mistake, he rose and fled without pausing to explain !

And as with social so with literary matters, he was always most at home with children and most ready and anxious to please them. *Phantasmagoria* was intended for grown-ups, but *Through the Looking-Glass* was on the way, and other stories were beginning to take shape in his mind. For when *Alice in Wonderland* had been out for not much more than a year, he had written another, very much shorter story for children, called " Bruno's Revenge," which he sent to Mrs. Gatty, the mother of Juliana Horatia Ewing, who was then editing *Aunt Judy's Magazine*, one of the best and most famous periodicals for children ever to appear. " I need hardly tell you that the story is *delicious,"* wrote Mrs. Gatty. " It is beautiful and fantastic and child-like, and I cannot sufficiently thank you. . . Make this one of a series. You may have great mathematical abilities, but so have hundreds of others. This talent is peculiarly your own, and as an Englishman you are almost unique in possessing it. . . " " As an Englishman," for Mrs. Gatty held that Hans Andersen was Dodgson's only serious rival.

And Mrs. Gatty continued to urge him to write more stories in the same series : in 1870 he is writing to her : " I was flattered to see that various of your correspondents (in *Aunt Judy*) wanted to hear again from Mr. Lewis Carroll —I should much enjoy telling them a little more about Bruno, if only I could find time and inventive faculty for it. . . "

It was a number of years before he actually found the time

necessary for making "Bruno's Revenge" into the two large volumes of *Sylvie and Bruno*, but from the time *Through the Looking-Glass* was finished, he was always collecting scraps of material for his next book, and storing up verses and burlesque poems which might be useful for it.

One of these humorous poems had an odd birth and an unexpected fate. Dodgson tells of its beginnings himself : " I was walking on a hill-side, alone, one bright summer day, when suddenly there came into my head one line of verse—one solitary line—' For the Snark *was* Boojum, you see.' I knew not what it meant, then : I know not what it means, now ; but I wrote it down : and, some time afterwards, the rest of the stanza occurred to me, that being its last line : and so by degrees, at odd moments during the next year or two, the rest of the poem pieced itself together, that being its last stanza. . ." By the summer of 1875 he had written three cantos, or " fits " as he called them, and had the idea of having it printed privately as a pamphlet with three illustrations by a new friend of his, the artist and sculptor Henry Holiday.

Dodgson had first met Holiday about six years earlier when the artist was staying in Oxford to paint the frieze in Worcester College chapel. Holiday's particular friend at Oxford was Dean Kitchen, whose little girl, Alexandra (always known as Xie) was one of Dodgson's favourite child-friends : she was a very beautiful child and he took particular pleasure in photographing her.

" Do you know how to obtain excellence in a photograph ? " Dodgson asked Holiday one day ; and when the artist proved unable to answer the riddle, he was told to " take a lens and put Xie before it ! "

Holiday stayed with Dodgson at Christ Church more than once in the next few years ; and in the summer of 1875 Dodgson paid a return visit to the artist's home in London, where he took a whole album full of photographs of Holiday and his family, of the children of the Marquis of Salisbury, and the actress Marion Terry in a suit of chain armor; and later in the year he had the prints mounted in a beautifully bound book which he presented to his host "In memory of a pleasant week."

It was shortly after this that Dodgson sent him three "fits" of *The Snark*, and Holiday, very much impressed by the strange medley of inspired nonsense, began at once to make rough sketches which he sent off to the author. But meanwhile Dodgson had written another "fit"—and dispatched it in haste to Holiday to be supplied with an illustration, and continued doing this—fitfully—until there were eight in all, making, with the frontispiece, nine elaborate pictures. There was a tenth picture, showing the Boojum itself, annihilating the Baker—but Dodgson, while being most impressed by the monster, said that the picture could not possibly appear in the book; "all his descriptions of the Boojum were quite unimaginable, and he wanted the creature to remain so." Some readers, nevertheless, insist that they can see the Boojum quite plainly in the last picture of the book, the one called "Then, silence"; but as none of them seem ever to have "softly and suddenly vanished away," one is forced to conclude that the shadowy monster must be a Snark of another kind—perhaps the portmanteau creature made of Shark and Snake, which Dodgson himself suggested was the origin of his own Snark—but certainly not the true Boojum of the poem.

Having prolonged the "Agony" into eight "Fits," Dodgson decided to publish *The Hunting of the Snark* as a slim book, and requested Holiday to devise some design for the cover. A year or two earlier the artist had made a sketch of a peculiar "Bell-buoy" in the sea off Land's End, and now he reproduced this accurate portrait, only weaving the words "It was a Boojum" into the original iron work.

On March 29, 1876, the book appeared, and although it was not received quite so enthusiastically as *Alice*, it yet became a favorite and still takes a good second place in most readers' affection. While many children do read it again and again (and one little girl learnt the whole poem by heart and insisted on reciting it to Dodgson during a railway journey!), it is really far more of a nonsense poem for grown-ups, and for some reason has always been a particular favorite of University professors and students —even before Dodgson's death, when it was the fashion among undergraduates to consider it as one of the great works of literature and also, it is said, of philosophy! Even now we find the hero of Mr. C. S. Lewis's romance *Perelandra* reciting it, together with chunks of the world's greatest epics, during one of his most trying adventures on the planet Venus. Yet of its meaning Dodgson himself wrote: "Periodically I have received courteous letters from strangers, begging to know whether *The Hunting of the Snark* is an allegory, or contains some hidden moral, or is a political satire: and for all such questions I have but one answer: '*I do not know!*' . . ." And later still he wrote: "I'm very much afraid I didn't mean anything but nonsense! Still, you know, words mean more than we mean to express when we use them; so a whole book ought to mean a great deal more than the writer means!", and when a lady wrote to the papers, declaring that the whole poem was "an allegory on the search after happiness," he was quite ready to admit that it might be so. But he would have been very upset had he known that his old friend Gabriel Rossetti, then nearing the end of his life with his mind slightly deranged by overdoses of drugs, considered it to be a bitter hidden attack on himself and his works as poet and painter.

But the *Snark* can neither be explained nor described: one can only read and re-read it, revelling in all or parts of it ; in the delightful Baker who had forgotten his luggage, his spare clothes, and his name, but "would answer to 'Hi!' or to any loud cry"; the Butcher, who could only kill Beavers, the Beaver who "appeared unaccountably shy" whenever the Butcher came near him ; in the logical nonsense (or is it nonsensical logic ?) of the Bellman, their Captain, who "had only one notion for crossing the ocean, And that was to tinkle his bell"; the ship itself, in which "the bowsprit got mixed with the rudder sometimes"; (you must read Dodgson's delightfully serious preface to find how this came about); but most of all the descriptions of the Snark, who can be known by "the taste, which is meager and hollow, but crisp," who gets up so late that it "frequently breakfasts at five o'clock tea, And dines on the following day." Then there is the sad fate of the Banker who meets a Bandersnatch :

"So great was his fright that his waistcoat turned white," in consequence of which,

"To the horror of all who were present that day,
He up rose in full evening dress!"

And finally the best method of Snark-hunting :

"You may seek it with thimbles—and seek it with care ;
You may hunt it with forks and hope ;
You may threaten its life with a railway share ;
You may charm it with smiles and soap."

With regard to hunting it "with forks and hope," you may be surprised to see Hope herself joining in the hunt in one of the pictures : Dodgson himself was just as surprised to see her there, and wrote to Holiday suggesting that he had missed the point—namely that "with" had a double job to perform, being used both with the instrument, "forks," and the mental attitude,"hope"; but Holiday wrote back triumphantly that he was working "with" even harder by using it in its third sense, "in company

114

with,"—to which Dodgson agreed, and both Hope and Care were allowed to join the hunt.

The many kinds of forks with which the party is hunting the Snark must also have pleased Dodgson, for it almost suggested some such amusement for children as " puzzle : who can find the most forks." But in devising games, puzzles and riddles Dodgson needed no assistance from anyone.

The earliest games were *Castle Croquet* and *Court Circular*, and were invented for Alice Liddell and her sisters. Both of these games must often have been played, but another, called *Circular Billiards*, can only have been played in the mathematical mind of its maker—for it needs a *round* billiards-table, and the whole interest in it centers in the unusual angles at which a ball would cannon off a curved cushion !

A more possible game was *Lanrick*, which is played on a chess-board with eight " draughts " men or " pawns " on each side and nine pieces of card cut to the size of a square. The rules are too long and complicated to describe here, and they have been reprinted once or twice ; but a game which, if it was published at all, appeared only in one or two newspapers in March, 1894, and has never been reprinted, is *Co-operative Backgammon* of which he gave the manuscript of the rules to a child-friend, Edith Lucy.

" Mr. Lewis Carroll . . . takes this opportunity to present his readers with the rules for *Co-operative Backgammon*, which he has just invented, and which he believes will prove to be an interesting variety of the Game, needing a good deal of thought and skill. *Rule I :* Each player throws *three* dice, and plays two of them for himself, and then the third for his adversary. *Rule II :* When no one of the three dice is available for the adversary, the player may use any two he likes ; otherwise, he must choose his 2 so as to leave one with which he can play for his adversary."

115

Much more popular were his word games, particularly *Doublets*, which became quite " the rage " when it appeared in the magazine *Vanity Fair* in 1879 ; this was before the days of Cross-word Puzzles for which, though he did not actually invent them, Dodgson laid all the foundations in this game, in another called *Syzygies*, and in his more and more complicated Acrostics and Anagrams.

The game of Doublets consists in changing one word into another of equal length ; this is done by means of a " chain " of words (the shorter the chain the better) changing one letter only at a time but always making a real word in the process. Thus " Make FLOUR into BREAD " (five links needed in the chain)—is done like this: "FLOUR, floor, flood, blood, brood, broad, BREAD." It is a pleasant, not very hard game to play, and experiment will show how difficult it is to stop when once one has begun to weave chains of words !

The next game, *Syzygies*, is even more complicated than its name, and can never have been popular, though *Syzygy* competitions were set in a magazine called *The Lady* during 1892. The method consists in " yoking " (which is what *Syzygy* means in Greek) two words together, but this time by chains made up of links consisting of as many letters as possible : thus W A L R U S, pe*ruse*, *harp*er, C A R P E N T E R. But there are pages of rules and methods of scoring, and only a mathematician can have taken much pleasure in it.

Yet another word game, *Misch-Masch* (named after the old family magazine of the Croft Rectory days) resembles *Syzygies* ; each side proposes a " nucleus " of two or more letters (say *emo*) and the other side provides a word containing the nucleus (say *lemons*) ; there are seven rules, including a system of marks for results. The game first appeared in *The Monthly Packet*, but did not prove very popular, and indeed one doubts whether any of these games, except the ever delightful *Doublets*, can have appealed to more than a few people. Dodgson himself realised this, for he wrote to one child, Edith Jebb : " You will find this puzzle (one of the games) very soothing : what the doctors call ' an alterative,' i.e., if you happen to have a headache, it will charm it away : but if you haven't one, it will probably give you one."

Much more entertaining, though even more mathematical, is *A Tangled Tale*, which is a series of stories of an amusing nature, each one containing a problem. There are ten " knots " in the Tangled Tale, and they all appeared in Charlotte Yonge's magazine *The Monthly Packet* between 1880 and 1885, where the readers were invited to unravel them : many of their answers being included in the book itself, which was published in 1885 with amusing illustrations by Arthur Frost who earlier had drawn the pictures for *Phantasmagoria*.

Clever too was *The Game of Logic*, which taught Logic, by means of counters on a board. Towards the end of his life Dodgson became more and more interested in Logic, carrying on long and learned controversies with various experts ; but he also taught, by means of such games as this, the girls at the Oxford High School and even the women Undergraduates at St. Hugh's and Lady Margaret Hall, both of which were flourishing before the end of his life. His last book of any importance was an easy introduction to Logic for young students (published over the name of " Lewis Carroll ") and he had a second and a third part planned out to complete the work.

Besides games and logical problems, Dodgson took great delight in inventing puzzles, riddles and charades. Puzzle-problems, or " conundrums " as they were usually called in those days, naturally attracted him as a mathematician, and during sleepless nights he would work out odd and complicated problems in arithmetic, algebra and even geometry. Among the " numerical curiosities " which he invented or discovered is one sufficiently simple and entertaining to be quoted here : " Put down any number of pounds not more than twelve, any number of shillings under twenty, and any number of pence under twelve. Under the pounds put the number of pence, under the shillings the number of shillings, and under the pence the number of pounds, thus reversing the line. Subtract. Reverse the line again. Add. Answer, £12 18s. 11d., *whatever* numbers may have been selected." This is well worth trying—and is much better than the old catch beginning : " Think of a number. . . " It is, by the way, advisable to choose a number of pence less than the number of pounds, so as to avoid minus quantities.

The most usual sort of conundrum was the riddle, and of these Dodgson had a good store, though unfortunately very few of them are recorded. The most famous is that asked by the Mad Hatter : " Why is a raven like a writing desk ? " There was, of course, no answer to it, but so many people asked Dodgson for one, that at last he suggested that a raven was like a writing-desk because both of them can produce a few notes, though these are almost always flat.

On June 30, 1892, he recorded in his diary : " Invented what I think is a new kind of riddle. A Russian had three sons. The first, named Rab, became a lawyer ; the second, Ymra, became a soldier ; the third became a sailor. What was his name ? " It is not difficult to guess if you study the other two names with sufficient care !

Even more characteristic are the riddles in verse, where the long word of the answer is divided into syllables or sections to which various clues are given, as in a game of charades. Take, for example, the following :

" My First is singular at best :
    More plural is my Second :
My Third is far the pluralest—
    So plural-plural, I protest
    It scarcely can be reckoned !

My First is followed by a bird :
  My Second by believers
In magic art : my simple Third
Follows, too often, hopes absurd
  And plausible deceivers . . ."

There are four more verses, the last two giving clues for the completed word, which is " Imagination " ; the sections are " I," " Magi," " Nation," and it is straightforward enough to see how the " lights " give these words—except " My First is followed by a bird," which is exceedingly cunning—for of course " I " is followed by " J," and a Jay is certainly a bird !

Dodgson's interest in charades leads on naturally to his enthusiasm for the stage, and his encouragement of amateur theatricals amongst his friends at Oxford. In the 'Sixties drama was frowned upon by the University ; there was no official dramatic society, and one group, *The Shooting Stars*, was firmly suppressed as the result of a scandal. Under these circumstances it required some courage to produce a play, but nevertheless on November 1 and 2, 1871, Mrs. Hatch, the mother of Dodgson's child-friends Beatrice, Evelyn, Edith and Wilfred, not only put on a " double bill," but asked him to write a prologue, which he did at some length ; and a couple of years later wrote another one, this time to be spoken by Beatrice and Wilfred.

Another Oxford child who was devoted to acting was Edith Lucy ; early in 1894 she was concerned in a production of the *Taming of the Shrew* with an all-female cast, and Dodgson came to see it and wrote her a very careful and plain-spoken criticism of it : " I don't feel that we are on the sort of terms to make it necessary for me to say pretty things only . . . if I am to be of any use to you, I must be candid. Well, my candid opinion is that the performance was as a whole *very* poor . . . This was not the fault of the *acting*, nor of the *business*, nor of the actors' knowledge of their parts : it was simply and solely the fault of the bad *delivery*. With one (or perhaps two) exceptions, you have *all* to learn the elements of stage elocution. . . Most of the play was simply *gabbled*, and it was quite out of the ques-

ELLEN TERRY
Photograph by Lewis Carroll

tion for an audience, not familiar with the text, to follow and enjoy it. . . " And he goes on to detailed criticism of some of the actresses, and elaborates it in another letter.

Perhaps Dodgson was rather too particular about

elocution, on which he was never tired of advising his little actress friends; but this was partly due to the continual attempts which he made to overcome the stammer in his own speech, even to the extent of reading a scene from Shakespeare out loud every night for many years.

His interest in acting had been with him since his earliest years at Oxford, and he never missed the chance of going to London to see some particularly good play or production, visiting nearly every one in which Ellen Terry appeared, and frequently taking children with him and giving them the supreme treat of being taken " back-stage " afterwards to meet the famous actress. He first saw her in June, 1856, when, as a child, she was playing the little prince Mamilius in *A Winter's Tale* : " I can't remember when I didn't know him," she wrote, " he made a progress as the years went on through the whole family. Finally he gave *Alice* to my children. He was a splendid theatre-goer, and took the keenest interest in all the Lyceum productions, frequently writing to point out slips in the dramatist's logic which only he would ever have noticed ! He did not even spare Shakespeare . . ,", and on one occasion wrote a long and amusing letter suggesting how Hero, in *Much Ado About Nothing*, ought to have proved an alibi when accused by Don Pedro of talking to Borachio out of her bedroom window :
" When Claudio asks her :
  ' What man was he talked with you yesternight
    Out of your window betwixt twelve and one ? '
Why doesn't she reply :
  ' I talked with no man at that hour, my Lord.
    Nor was I in my chamber yesternight,
    But in another, far from it, remote.'
And this she could, of course, prove by the evidence of the housemaids, who must have known that she had occupied another room that night. . . If only there had been a

barrister present to cross-examine Beatrice! 'Now, ma'am, attend to me please, and speak up so that the jury can hear you. Where did you sleep last night? Where did Hero sleep? . . .' "

Later on in his life Dodgson began to make more and more friends among stage-children, helping them as much as he could to make a success of their careers, and helping them too in other ways, for the stage-child came usually of poor parents, and had very little time for education or culture.

And the real beginning of his particular interest in child actresses began in 1886 when *Alice* was first made into a play and produced in London.

CHAPTER VIII

CHILD-FRIENDS

THE two *Alice* books were turned into an " operetta " by Henry Savile Clarke, with music by Walter Slaughter in 1886; there were a number of songs in it, of which many were the original ones from the books, but at least half were verses of very little worth composed specially by the adapter. Indeed, although the play was made out of *Alice*, Dodgson with his usual modesty would never speak of himself as the author. " Not that the play itself is in any sense mine," he wrote. " The arrangements, in dramatic form, of a story written without the slightest idea that it would be so adapted, was a task that demanded powers denied to me, but possessed in an eminent degree, so far as I can judge, by Mr. Savile Clarke. I do not feel myself qualified to criticise his play, as a play. . . "

But in spite of this, he took an active interest in the production, attending some of the rehearsals, and writing at least one verse that was needed—the completion of " 'Tis the voice of the lobster." Of this poem there are four versions : in all editions of *Alice* up to 1886 appear only the first four lines of the first verse and the first two lines of the second verse (with an oyster in place of a panther) ; in 1870 the songs were reprinted separately with music by William Boyd, and for this Dodgson completed the second verse as follows :

" I passed by his garden, and marked, with one eye,
   How the owl and the oyster were sharing a pie ;
   While the duck and the Dodo, the lizard and cat
   Were swimming in milk round the brim of a hat."

In 1886 four more lines were added to the first verse, which are to be found in almost every edition since, and the second verse was re-written, also in eight lines which everyone knows well :

"I passed by his garden, and marked, with one eye,
    How the Owl and the Panther were sharing a pie ;
    The Panther took pie-crust, and gravy, and meat,
    While the Owl had the dish as its share of the treat.
    When the pie was all finished, the Owl, as a boon,
    Was kindly permitted to pocket the spoon :
    While the Panther received knife and fork with a growl,
    And concluded the banquet by — "

Here the Mock Turtle rudely interrupts with "What *is* the use of repeating all that stuff ? " but no one is left in any doubt that the last line should run :

"And concluded the banquet by eating the owl."

However, for the play (and probably it was written before the best and final version) the last two lines of the complete poem run :

"But the Panther obtained both the fork and the knife—
    And when *he* lost his temper, the owl lost its life."

It is doubtful how much "say" Dodgson had in the adaptation and preparation of the piece : he originally gave Savile Clarke permission to dramatise the books on condition that there should be "no *suggestion* even, of coarseness in libretto or in stage business," and this at least he would have seen to throughout. However, he went to see it as an ordinary member of the public on December 30, 1886, taking a child with him, and wrote of it in his diary : "The first act (Wonderland) goes well, specially the Mad Tea Party. Mr. Sydney Harcourt is a capital Hatter, and little Dorothy d'Alcourt (æt. $6\frac{1}{2}$) a delicious Dormouse. Phoebe Carlo is a splendid Alice. Her song and dance with the Cheshire Cat . . . was a gem. As a whole the play seems a success."

ROYAL GLOBE THEATRE.

Sole Lessee and Manager .. .. .. Mr RICHARD MANSFIELD

WEDNESDAY, DECEMBER 26th, 1888, and every Afternoon at 2.30,

ALICE IN WONDERLAND,

A MUSICAL DREAM PLAY, in Two Acts, for Children and others, founded on LEWIS CARROLL'S STORIES

By H. SAVILE CLARKE. Music by WALTER SLAUGHTER. Produced under the Direction of the AUTHOR and Mr. EDGAR BRUCE.

Incidental Dances arranged by Mdlle. ROSA. Properties by LABHART. Dresses by M. and Madame ALIAS, designed by M. L. BESCHE, from Mr.
JOHN TENNIEL'S Illustrations to the Stories. Entirely New Scenery.

A Nursery Magician cook	Ours is the task, with Elfin dance
All little children by the hand;	And song, to give to Childhood's gaze
And led them laughing through the book	That Wonderland; and should it chance
Where Alice walks in Wonderland.	To win a smile, be his the praise.
	H. Savile Clarke.

Act I.—ALICE'S ADVENTURES IN WONDERLAND.

Alice ... ... Miss ISA BOWMAN

White Rabbit ... ... Master CHARLES BOWMAN	Dormouse ... ... Miss EMMIE BOWMAN
Caterpillar ... ... Master JOHN SMART	King of Hearts ... Master STEPHEN ADESON
Duchess ... ... Miss NORTON	Queen of Hearts ... ... Miss DEWHURST
Cook ... ... Miss EDITH VANBRUGH	Knave of Hearts ... Miss IRENE VANBRUGH
Cheshire Cat ... Master CHARLES ADESON	Executioner ... ... Mr ROY
Hatter ... ... Mr. SIDNEY HARCOURT	Gryphon... ... ... Mr. DRUCE
Hare ... ... Mr GODFREY	Mock Turtle... ... Mr. T, P. HAYNES

Scenes: I.—A Forest in Autumn.   II.—Wonderland. (Mr. E. BANKS.)

Alice asleep—The Song of the Elves—Alice awakes in Wonderland—The White Rabbit—"How doth the Little Crocodile"—The Caterpillar—"You are
Old Father William"—The Duchess—The Baby and the Cook !

Speak roughly to your little boy   He only does it to annoy
And beat him when he sneezes.   Because he thinks it teases.

The Cheshire Cat—The March Hare—The Hatter and the Dormouse—The Mad Tea Party—"Twinkle, Twinkle, little Bat"—The Dormouse's Story—
"So they say"—The King and Queen of Hearts—The Knave of Hearts—"Off with her head"   GRAND GAVOTTE OF CARDS.
The Cheshire Cat again—A Cat may look at a King—The Cat ordered for Execution—"Can't be done"—Trio: "He is the Executioner"—The Mock
Turtle—The Gryphon—The Story of their School days "Beautiful Soup so rich and green"—The Lobster Quadrille—"Will you walk a little faster !"

'Tis the voice of the Lobster I heard him declare.   The Story of the Whiting—and the Porpoise.
You have baked me too brown, I must swear my hair;   As a duck with her eyelids, so he with his nose,
          Turns his belt and his buttons and turns out h' toes.

The Stolen Tarts—The Trial of the Knave of Hearts—The Hatter's Evidence—The Twinkling of the Tea—The Dormouse denies it—Alice's verdict—FINALE.

Act II.—THROUGH THE LOOKING-GLASS.

Alice ... ... Miss ISA BOWMAN

White King ... ... Mr GODFREY	Tweedledum ... ... Mr SIDNEY HARCOURT
White Queen ... Miss IRENE VANBRUGH	Tweedledee ... ... Mr. T. P. HAYNES
The Carpenter ... ... Mr. ROY	Humpty Dumpty ... ... Mr. DRUCE
The Walrus ... ... Mr. DRUCE	The Lion ... ... Master ALLWOOD
White Knight ... Master STEPHEN ADESON	The Unicorn ... Master CHARLES BOWMAN
Lily ... ... Miss NORTON	Hare ... ... Mr. GODFREY
Rose ... ... Miss EDITH VANBRUGH	Cook ... ... Mr. SMILES
Red Queen ... ... Miss DEWHURST	Plum Pudding ... ... Miss D'ALCOURT
Red King ... Master CHARLES ADESON	Oyster Ghost (with Hornpipe) ... Miss EMMIE BOWMAN

Scene — Looking-Glass Land. (Mr. E. BANKS.)

Looking-glass Land—The Chessmen and the Chorus—The Red King and the Red Queen—"Jabberwocky."
'Twas brillig and the slithy toves   All mimsy were the borogoves
Did gyre and gimble in the wabe   And the mome raths outgrabe.

Appearance of the Jabberwock—General consternation—The Garden of Live Flowers—What the Lily and Rose said—The Red Queen's advice—
Tweedledum and Tweedledee—"Here we go round the Mulberry Bush"—The Walrus and the Carpenter
The fate of the Oysters—The broken rattle—Great and deadly combat between Tweedledum and Tweedledee—The Crow and the Heroes—The White
Queen and jam every other day—The visit to Humpty-Dumpty and Alice's Interview with him—"an un-birthday present—The fall of Humpty-Dumpty
and " all the King's Horses and all the King's Men "—The Red King and the Anglo-Saxon Messenger.

THE LION AND THE UNICORN FIGHTING FOR THE CROWN —The White Knight—Alice becomes a Queen—The Festival.
Sound the festal trumpets, set the bells a-ringing,   Raise on high the chalice in our honour singing.
Here are curried trumpets, crocodiles, and beans!   Welcome, welcome, Alice, with the noble Queens

OH! I'VE HAD SUCH A CURIOUS DREAM."

PRICES—Private Boxes from £1 1s ; Stalls, 10s. 6d ; DressCircle 6s . Upper Boxes, 3s ; Pit, 2s ; Gallery, 1s.
SPECIAL REDUCED PRICES FOR CHILDREN UNDER TWELVE—Stalls, 5s. 6d ; Dress Circle, 3s.
Musical Director   Doors open at 2.15; Commence at 2.30. Box Office open from 10 to 5, under the direction of Mr. F, H. Jungs.
          Mr. EDWARD GERMAN   Stage Managers   ...   Mr. SIDNEY HARCOURT and Mr. E. B. NORMAN
Business Manager for "Alice in Wonderland"   ...   Mr. E. D. GRIFFITHS.

IMPERIAL-GRENADE FIRE EXTINGUISHERS are fitted up throughout this Theatre as a provision against Fire.
All ICES sold at this Theatre are supplied by the HORTON ICE CREAM Co., and Tea and Coffee by DAKIN & COMP'Y.

PROGRAMME OF *ALICE IN WONDERLAND* "OPERETTA"

Elsewhere Dodgson gave special praise to Harcourt's performance : " To see him enact the Hatter was a weird and uncanny thing, as though some grotesque monster, seen last night in a dream, should walk into the room in broad daylight " ; and professed himself best pleased of all with Dorothy d'Alcourt's Dormouse, " with her beaming baby-face, the delicious crispness of her speech, and the perfect realism with which she makes herself the embodied essence of sleep. . . With the first words of her opening speech, a sudden silence falls upon the house. . . And yet I doubt if the charm is due only to the incisive clearness of her articulation ; to me there was an even greater charm in the utter self-abandonment and conscientious *thoroughness* of her acting. . ."

One bit of stage " business " was certainly devised by Dodgson : he felt that in the Walrus and Carpenter scene it was not sufficiently exciting for the oysters merely to die quietly at the end, and so " he conceived the happy thought of making the ghosts of the victims jump on the sleeping forms of their assassins, and give them bad dreams " ; and he went on to tell the Oxford acquaintance who records this, " that the spirit shown by the defunct oysters in inflicting this (somewhat mild) retaliation drew loud applause from the spectators."

The ghost of the First Oyster was given by Savile Clarke a Mazurka to dance, and the following song to sing :
" The Carpenter is sleeping, the butter's on his face,
The Vinegar and Pepper are all about the place.
Let Oysters rock your cradle, and lull you into rest,
And if that will not do it, we'll sit upon your chest."

But the ghost of the Second Oyster, who danced the Horn-pipe, had no song to sing, and none was ever printed for her in the book of the play. Now the part was played either from the beginning, or shortly afterwards, by Dodgson's child-friend Nellie Bowman, and a little later by Nellie's younger sister, Empsie, and they were so disappointed at not having a song to sing, that Dodgson himself wrote a second verse specially for them—and almost sixty years later both of them could still remember the lines and sing them to me :

" Oh woeful, weeping Walrus, your tears are all a sham,
You're greedier for Oysters than children are for jam.
You'd like to have an Oyster to give your meal a zest ?
Excuse me, weeping Walrus, for stamping on your
    chest ! "

When the play had finished its London run it went on tour for many months all over the country, and it was still being performed when Dodgson went to see it at Brighton on July 15 (1887). By this time he had three particular friends in the company, including one or two at least of the Bowman sisters, all of whom he knew well by the end of that year, Isa the eldest becoming before long the favorite of all his child-friends at any time and almost his adopted niece.

At that time many people were writing letters to the papers about children on the stage, saying what a bad effect acting had upon them, the " physical strain " and the " fatal results " caused by the hardness of the life. Dodgson did not agree, declared that over-work in a Board School produced far more fatal results, and wrote to *The St. James' Gazette*, the best evening paper of the day, describing what must have been a typical afternoon with children at the seaside :

" I spent yesterday afternoon at Brighton, where for five hours I enjoyed the society of three exceedingly happy and healthy little girls, aged twelve, ten and seven. We paid three visits to the houses of friends ; we spent a long time on the pier . . . and invested pennies in every mechanical device which invited such contributions and promised anything worth having, for body or mind, in return : we even made an excited raid on headquarters, like Shylock with three attendant Portias, to demand the 'pound of flesh'— in the form of a box of chocolate drops—which a dyspeptic machine had refused to render. I think that anyone who could have seen the vigour of *life* in these three children— the intensity with which they enjoyed everything, great or small, which came in their way—who could have watched the younger two running races on the Pier, or could have heard the fervent exclamation of the eldest at the end of the afternoon, 'We *have* enjoyed ourselves!' would have agreed with me that here indeed was no excessive 'physical strain,' nor any imminent danger of 'fatal results'! . . . A drama, written by Mr. Savile Clarke, is now being played at Brighton: and in this (it is called *Alice in Wonderland*) all three children have been engaged, with only a month's interval, ever since Christmas: the youngest being Dormouse, as well as three other characters—the second appearing, though not in a speaking part—while the elder plays the heroine, Alice—quite the heaviest part in the whole play, and, I should think, the heaviest ever undertaken by a child; she has no less than 215 speeches! They have been acting every night this week, and *twice* on the day before I met them, the second performance lasting until after half-past ten at night—after which they got up at seven next morning to bathe! . . . "

It was at the sea-side that Dodgson began so many of his friendships with children, going each year to stay in Eastbourne as if with the express idea of such meetings.

Dodgson was a most careful and methodical traveller, and gave just as much care and forethought to each of his journeys as he did to every other detail of his life. When he set out he carried only one little black bag with him, but his luggage—a great number of suitcases—had all been sent on ahead, every article in them wrapped up carefully in a separate piece of paper. In his pocket he carried two large purses, each specially made, with a great number of pockets and divisions in them, so that he could carry separately the exact amount of money which he would need at each stage of his journey—so much for a cab, so much for a ticket, so much for a paper, so much to tip the porter, and so on to his journey's end. Once seated in his first-class compartment—a non-smoker, for he did not himself smoke, and in those days no lady either smoked or would travel in a smoking compartment—he would wait hopefully, looking at his fellow travellers, until some child should get in with her mother. And if this happened, or if he were able to choose a compartment in which a child was already settled, Dodgson wasted no time in beginning to make friends. Out of the black bag would come puzzles, picture books, paper and pencils, and Dodgson would tell stories, illustrating them with rough drawings as he went along, and writing verses, charades or riddles ; and before the journey ended he would get the name and address of his new child-friend, and a few days later she received a copy of *Alice*, and perhaps a delightful nonsense letter which finally revealed who he was.

One day he was in the same carriage with a lady and her little daughter who were both complete strangers to him, and they were reading *Alice in Wonderland*. Dodgson began to talk to the little girl about the book, and presently her mother, who had no idea whatsoever to whom she was talking, said : " Isn't it sad about poor Mr. Lewis Carroll ? He's gone mad, you know." " Indeed," replied Dodgson, much interested, " I had never heard that." " Oh, I assure you it's quite true," she continued, " I have it on the best authority." Before the end of the journey Dodgson promised to send a present to the little girl, and a few days later she received a copy of *Through the Looking-Glass*, inscribed with her name and " From the Author, in memory of a pleasant journey."

Many other friendships with children began at the sea-side ; Dodgson was accustomed to sit on the shore with his pockets full of safety-pins and games : when some little girl was in difficulties about keeping her frock out of the water while she went paddling, he would gravely present her with the necessary pins ; and when the child had finished paddling, she usually came back to him, and he would produce the puzzles, or begin to tell stories to her. One such " sea-shore " child was Gertrude Chataway, whose name you may find twice over in the dedication poem in front of the *Hunting of the Snark :* " We used to sit for hours," she wrote, " on the wooden steps which led from our garden on to the beach, whilst he told the most lovely tales that could possibly be imagined, often illustrating the exciting situations with a pencil as he went along. . . It was the most lovely nonsense conceivable, and I naturally revelled in it. His imagination would fly from one subject to another, and he was never tied down in any way by the probabilities of life. To *me* it was of course all perfect, but it is astonishing that *he* never seemed either tired, or to want other society. . . "

But Oxford showed Dodgson at his best, and in his true surroundings, and it is there that most of his particular child-friends knew him and that we who know him only through his writings and their memories can best picture him.

Take a typical Oxford day in the early eighteen-eighties—one of those perfect days at the end of October when the sun shines until the yellow towers and spires glow like honey against the pale blue of the sky. It is afternoon and the mist is creeping over the Meadows and the Parks where the long grass goes down to the river's edge and the gaunt trees are shedding their last pale leaves. In the frosty air ring the merry voices of children, and their feet echo from the hard clay and gravel of the frozen paths as they return home after the afternoon walk. Suddenly one of them sees, in the distance the tall figure in black, clerical clothes and a top hat " swinging along towards the little group with a characteristic briskness, almost jauntiness, of step. At once, long before his face is visible, she recognises him, and shouts with excitement. ' It's Uncle Dodgson! Here comes Uncle Dodgson! Let's make a barrier across the path so that he can't pass!' " Less fortunate children on less fortunate days if they had only seen him across the road and been waved to, would come home bursting with excitement: "I saw Mr. Dodgson today!"; but this time fortune is favoring them. Dodgson also appreciates the situation; as they join hands and form a line across the path, he comes charging down upon them with his umbrella at the " ready." The line breaks in confusion, and in a moment the children are clinging to him wherever they can obtain a hold and shrieking with delight. Presently the excitement dies down, and they go on, hand in hand with him, chatting merrily.

After that, one or two of them are invited to have tea with him and set off through the twilight towards Christ Church. In they go, still hanging firmly on to his hands, under the bell-tower where " Big Tom " is perhaps striking four o'clock; turn left at once, up the steps on to the wide stone terrace which runs right round the great quadrangle, and along to the last door on the left before the corner. No. 7 staircase it is, where he lived from November, 1868, until his death, and they go up the steep winding old stairs until they reach the heavy black door over which is painted in big white letters " The Rev. C. L. Dodgson." Beyond this is a passage with shelves of books, and at the end of it a door with glass panels which opens into the large, lofty, cheerful sitting room. There is a fire burning brightly in the fireplace in the same wall as the door, and the windows on the right which look out on to a private garden, and in

131

front which overlook St. Aldate's, still show the gray of the evening light. On either side of this big oriel window are two little turret rooms with windows of their own ; they are hardly more than alcoves, but Dodgson used to promise little Isa Bowman that if, when she got married, she and her husband should ever quarrel, he would let them come and live one in each of these little rooms !

Meanwhile, Dodgson lights the big lamps, draws the crimson damask window-curtains, and pulls up the couch with its red " rep " cushions still nearer to the fire. The children look round them with awe and wonder at the room where " Lewis Carroll " writes his stories ; all round the walls are shelves full of books, and below the shelves great cupboards where are kept an incredible collection of toys and other thrilling objects; there are mechanical bears and dancing dolls, there is Leotard the acrobat on his bar, there are puzzles and devices of every sort and description, musical-boxes, conjuring tricks, sets for chess, draughts and backgammon, microscopes, telescopes, and a hundred and one other novelties. Hanging over the mantelpiece are three portraits of child-friends, " the one in the middle being a picture of a little girl in a blue coat and cap, who is carrying a pair of skates." In the middle of the room is a big, mahogany table, and to one side a tall pine-wood desk at which Dodgson stands to write. One remarkable thing is the tidiness of the room ; papers and manuscripts are piled high on shelves and tables, but every pile is arranged neatly, is numbered, and is ready for use at a moment's notice. The manuscript lying on the desk is written most clearly and carefully, usually in violet ink— and no printer (this is before the days of typewriters) would ever have a moment's bother over " setting up " Mr. Lewis Carroll's latest book.

On another desk—probably a folding desk of the kind that one puts on to a table—are Mr. Dodgson's materials

DODGSON'S STUDY AT CHRIST CHURCH, OXFORD

for writing letters. There is the " letter-register," which contained 98,404 entries at the time of his death (he began it on January 1, 1861), in which he enters every letter written or received, together with dates and a short precis of contents ; there is his note-paper, nearly a dozen different sized sheets : " Let me see," he would say before beginning a letter, " size so-and-so will be about right for this ! "— and it always was. Another little device which he invented was the " Wonderland Postage Stamp Case," a little card-board folder in an envelope with pockets inside for every value of stamp, and " surprise " pictures from *Alice* on the outside—Alice with the baby, which has turned into a pig when you pull out the folder, and the Cheshire Cat " as large as life " on the envelope, and " twice as natural " on the folder where only its grin remains. With the case went a little booklet called *Eight or Nine Wise Words about Letter Writing*, containing much serious wisdom, and a few amusing remarks : " . . . Postage-Stamp-Cases may be divided into one class, the ' Wonderland ' . . . This case is *not* intended to carry about in your pocket. . . No, *this* is meant to haunt your envelope-case, or wherever you keep your writing materials. . . My second Rule is, don't fill *more* than a page and a half with apologies for not having written sooner. . . A postscript is a very useful invention, but it is *not* meant (as so many ladies suppose) to contain the real *gist* of the letter . . . ", and so on.

But there is no more time for looking about the room, because Uncle Dodgson is now making the tea, and asking you to admire his kettle, " all my own invention." Most people, he would say, either burnt their hands on kettles, or used kettle-holders which were always dirty and usually lost ; but he had got a blacksmith to attach to his own kettle a long handle like that on a saucepan, by means of which he could lift it off the fire in complete comfort, and fill the teapot. This once performed and the story of his invention told, he then proceeds to walk up and down on the hearth-rug gravely swinging the teapot from side to side for exactly ten minutes so that it shall " draw " properly. While infusing the tea he usually talked to his visitors, telling them stories, perhaps of other child-friends or, if they were a trifle older, of the autograph-hunters who had been plaguing him lately, and of how he would either send a printed note (" Mr. Dodgson . . . neither claims nor acknowledges any connection with any pseudonym, or with any book that is not published under his own name. Having therefore no claim to retain, or even to read the enclosed, he returns it for the convenience of the writer who has thus mis-addressed it") ; or else get someone else to write the letter, and then ask some friend or colleague to sign " Lewis Carroll " for him : it was always a matter of great amusement to imagine what these tiresome correspondents would think if ever they came to compare the various " Lewis Carroll " autographs, all of which were so obviously by a different hand !

After tea (or after dinner, in the case of slightly older child-friends : and dinner, or a grown-up dinner-party, would be served in Dodgson's small sitting room, the dishes placed on squares of cardboard, as he considered mats a waste of money, and great care taken—by means of lists and diagrams—that the same guest should never have the same meal, or sit next to the same person twice) they would settle down by the fire. This was in the earlier years, for later he limited his guests severely to one at a time ; and a party came to consist of a young lady rather than a child, to share his own frugal supper, for by then he had outgrown his shyness of grown-up girls—and the legend that he was not interested in anyone older than twelve or fourteen was only true of his younger days. A small child was entertained first of all with some of the mechanical toys :

"Isa, my darling," he would say, "once upon a time there was someone called Bob the Bat! And he lived in the top left-hand drawer of the writing table. What could he do when uncle wound him up?"

And Isa exclaimed, breathless with excitement, "He could really FLY!"

Bob was wound up by means of elastic, and darted eerily about the room, just a little bit alarming to a very young or nervous child.

And when these joys were exhausted Dodgson would turn to the musical boxes, of which he had a very large number, and he and the children sit listening gravely to their tunes. Sometimes one of them stuck, and then he would go to a drawer in the table and produce a box of little screw-drivers and punches, and, with Isa still sitting on his knee, unscrew the lid and take out the wheels to see what was the matter. And if "butter wouldn't suit the works," he was quite ready to put them in back to front so that the music began from the end and played tunes the wrong way round! Or else he might get out the "orguinette" (which was like a miniature "pianola") and putting in roll after roll, all of which were carefully catalogued, turn the handle solemnly, raising and lowering the lid to vary the sound, his favourite tune being one called "Santa Lucia."

And then would come stories in wonderful variety: there was one which Evelyn Hatch recollected particularly "which finished with the words: 'My dear, you are a *Perfect Goose!*' and lo! and behold, the drawing which had gone alongside the tale of a little man and woman who lived in a house with one window, by the side of a lake, and had been frightened by imaginary burglars, was turned upside down and there was a *Perfect Goose!* It was the way Mr. Dodgson told it, rather than the story itself, which always gave the never-to-be-forgotten thrill."

Other stories were inspired by the picture tiles which Dodgson had made specially and put round the fireplace; these represented the ship out of *The Hunting of the Snark*, the Beaver, the Dodo, the Eaglet and a bird transfixing a fish; in between the picture tiles were others on which were a variety of strange creatures that seem to be birds. " As I sat on Mr. Dodgson's knee before the fire," wrote Enid Stevens, " he used to let the creatures have long and very amusing conversations between themselves. The little creatures on the intervening tiles used to squirm in at intervals. I think they suggested the ' Little Birds are Feeding ' verses in *Sylvie and Bruno*."

Towards the end of his life Dodgson made friends with a number of older girls, including students from the women's colleges, St. Hugh's and Lady Margaret Hall, as here he used occasionally to lecture on Logic. In his case alone the firm rule of those days about young women never going out without a " chaperone " was always dropped (and Dodgson was most offended if anyone even suggested that it was improper for a young lady to dine alone with him in his rooms) ; at the women's colleges " chaperonage " was very strictly enforced—but even there an exception was made in his favor.

"I only like a *tete-a-tete* dinner," he would say, "And if you don't come alone, you shan't come at all ! "

And Miss Moberly, the Principal of St. Hugh's, would smile sweetly when the girl came, letter in hand, to ask her permission, and say : " Once more, we must make a virtue of necessity ! "

The invitation accepted, Dodgson would turn up sharp at 6.30 at St. Hugh's, and conduct his guest back to Christ Church in time for dinner at 7 o'clock, and he used to say that these walks, and the return journey in the evening, which was timed to reach St. Hugh's at 10.30 exactly (a rule of which he *did* approve), were the best part of his dinner-parties.

Once in his rooms they would sit down immediately to a supper which never altered—well cooked mutton chops followed by meringues, followed by a glass or two of port (which surely Dodgson did not allow his girl-friend to drink !), and tea an hour or so later, after a pleasant conversation ranging from children to Logic.

Of all his child-friends, however, the very favourite was Isa Bowman, who acted the part of *Alice* in 1888, when the play was revived with others of Dodgson's child-friends in the cast—Charles and Empsie Bowman, Edith and Irene Vanbrugh, and Nellie Bowman understudying and playing part of the time. Isa used to come and stay with him at Eastbourne during his summer holidays, and he more or less adopted her, attending to her education and even helping her with her stage career.

" At Eastbourne," she writes, " I was happier even with Lewis Carroll than I was at Oxford. We seemed more free, and there was the air of a holiday over it all. Every day of my stay at the house in Lushington Road [it was No. 7] was a perfect dream of delight."

In the mornings they used to get up very early indeed, and Isa, who was usually ready first, would wait quietly outside her bedroom until Dodgson was ready ; as soon as he was, he pushed a newspaper under his door, and directly she saw it Isa would come bursting in to kiss him good morning. Then they went down to breakfast, and after that Dodgson read out loud a chapter of the Bible, and Isa had to re-tell it to him in her own words to make sure that she had understood it.

" Now then, Isa dearest," he used to say, " tell me a story and mind you begin with ' Once upon a time.' A story which does not begin with ' Once upon a time ' can't possibly be a good story. It's *most* important."

The story ended, they would set out from the house, Isa to the swimming bath, once she had promised to make the almost daily visit to the dentist which Dodgson considered necessary, immediately afterwards. When this was done, it was time to return for lunch, at which Dodgson, much to Isa's continuous anxiety, would never eat more than a biscuit and drink a glass of sherry.

" Aren't you hungry, uncle, even *today?* " she used to ask.

After lunch came a lesson in backgammon, which was his favorite game for many years, and then the long afternoon walk on to Beachy Head, which Isa disliked so. Dodgson, however, believed in exercise and thought that one should always go to bed physically tired from the exercise of the day, so as not to suffer from sleeplessness to which he himself was most liable. On the way he told stories and invented games to make the walk less of a penance for Isa, and when she was tired they would sit down to rest while he made wonderful things out of his handkerchief, including the usual jumping mouse, at which he was very expert.

When they actually arrived at the top of Beachy Head, tea was waiting for them at the coastguard's cottage— though Dodgson would never allow Isa to take more than one rock cake and one cup of tea. And then came stories as they sat on the grass looking out over the sea—fairy tales, strange romances about deep, dark woods and great scaly dragons, or stories of Dodgson's own experiences, particularly of how he once got lost on Beachy Head in a thick fog and was forced to feel his way home by means of the boulders.

" Just as the sun was setting," related Isa, " and a cool breeze whispered round us, he would take off his hat and let the wind play with his hair, and he would look out to sea. Once I saw tears in his eyes, and when we turned to go he gripped my hand much tighter than usual."

But if Isa enjoyed the visits to Eastbourne best of all, she was also very pleased when " Uncle Charles " (as she alone seems to have called him) invited her to stay in Oxford. There she used to lodge in a little house just outside the college gates, and come in to Christ Church to spend her days with Dodgson.

One particular visit which she paid him in July 1888 he celebrated by writing a diary for her called *Isa's visit to Oxford*, a most amusing and charming little composition, which unfortunately is much too long to include here. It describes all the places they visited and the things they did —exploring the various colleges, playing games, meeting people, and so on. Sometimes it merges over into real " Lewis Carroll " nonsense, as when Isa puts the roll into the " orguinette " wrong end first, with the result that they " had a tune backwards, and soon found themselves in the day before yesterday : so they dared not go on, for fear of making Isa so young she would not be able to talk." And each chapter ends with a fanciful account of what Isa dreamed that night in consequence of all she had seen and done during the day : for example, " Isa went to bed, and dreamed she was buzzing about among the flowers with the dear Gorilla : but there wasn't any honey in them—only slices of bread-and-butter, and multiplication-tables."

And when Isa's sister, Maggie, came to Oxford in June, 1889, on tour in a play, Dodgson wrote her a little diary, but in verse this time, beginning :

> " When Maggie once to Oxford came
>   On tour as ' Bootles' Baby,'
> She said ' I'll see this place of fame,
>   However dull the day be ! '
>
> So with her friend she visited
>   The sights that it was rich in :
> And first of all she poked her head
>   Into the Christ Church Kitchen . . ."

They were very happy days spent wandering about Oxford

CHARLES DODGSON, AGED 56
Photograph taken at Guildford about 1888

with so wonderful a companion as Charles Dodgson ; but, recalls Isa, " I think I was almost happiest when we came back to his rooms and had tea alone ; when the fire-glow (it was always winter when I stayed in Oxford) threw fantastic shadows about the quaint room, and the thoughts of the prosiest of people must have wandered a little into fancyland. The shifting firelight seemed almost to etherealise that kindly face, and as the wonderful stories fell from his lips, and his eyes lighted on me with the sweetest smile that ever a man wore, I was conscious of a love and reverence for Charles Dodgson that became nearly an adoration."

CHAPTER IX

SYLVIE AND BRUNO

OF Charles Dodgson's life after he settled at Christ Church there is hardly anything more to tell : year followed year with peaceful regularity, in term-time the mathematical lectures were given without a break until he resigned his lectureship in 1881 so as to have more time for writing ; the mathematical books appeared at intervals, uninterrupted by the publication of the works of " Lewis Carroll " ; the summer holiday was spent at the sea-side, at Eastbourne from about 1880 onwards, and Christmas with his sisters at Guildford ; there were expeditions to a theatre in London, usually with a child ; there were the long walks out of Oxford ; there were the child-friends who came to tea, and the girl undergraduates who came to dinner —all these things happening year after year with very little variation, just as I have already described them.

Indeed, very few things ever happened to Charles Dodgson ; but however quiet and uneventful his own existence was, his mind was always turning to new things, and he died long before he had written all the books which he had planned to write even as early as March 29, 1885, when he lists them in his diary : besides many works on mathematics and Logic, these include *A Tangled Tale*, *Original Games and Puzzles*, *The Nursery Alice*, serious Poems, *Alice's Adventures Underground*, *Girl's Own Shakespeare*, *Sylvie and Bruno*, a drama on *Alice* and a volume of theological essays.

The Nursery Alice was published in 1889, consisting of many incidents from the actual book very simply and charmingly retold by Dodgson for children "from o to 5", printed in large type, with some of Tenniel's illustrations, also enlarged and colored by his friend Gertrude Thomson. Dodgson always professed to dislike small children—but it was really only babies for whom he did not care, and when fond mothers held up their squealing offspring for him to admire, he would remark gravely: "He *is* a baby!" Perhaps this was also rather a "pose," just as his dislike of small boys seems to have been; he certainly enjoyed exaggerating his sentiments about babies, for he wrote to Ethel Arnold in 1884 about the expedition to Woodstock on which he wanted her to accompany him: "There is a baby there to be admired—about two years old I think, and in this matter you will be of incalculable service to me, and relieve me of all responsibility as to saying the proper thing when animals of that kind are offered for inspection."

Alice's Adventures Underground, which came out in 1886, was a facsimile of the orginal story which he had written out so long ago for Alice Liddell. Now he borrowed it from her and had each page photographed carefully just as it was, with all his own drawings; only the last page was changed, and for that he wrote a little slip to go over the photo of Alice. Of the other "Projects," the serious poems appeared just after his death as *Three Sunsets*, being almost entirely those which had been included years before in *Phantasmagoria*; and of course the "drama on Alice" was written by Savile Clarke. Dodgson always wanted to write plays, but although years earlier he wrote to Tom Taylor the dramatist asking his advice on a domestic comedy which he was trying to compose, he never seems to have completed one. None of the other books were ever finished—though *Original Games and Puzzles* was announced by the publisher as "in preparation"—none, except of course Dodgson's last really important work, *Sylvie and Bruno*.

144

Out of every thousand people who have read *Alice*, probably only one has read *Sylvie and Bruno*, even in the shortened edition which was published some years after Dodgson's death ; and yet one would hardly say that *Alice* is a thousand times better ! *Sylvie and Bruno* is a difficult book, it is much too long, and it contains so many odd things jumbled together, that very few people can be bothered to wade through the parts which are usually considered dull. For although the construction of the book is exceedingly ingenious, many of the things put into it do not fit at all, and it is inclined to be spoilt as a fairy story by the grown-up novel which is combined with it—just as the grown-up novel loses so much of its force on account of the nonsense, however brilliant, which keeps creeping into it.

Why Dodgson wrote this extraordinary book in the way that he did, it is hard to say. His own idea was that as *Alice*, which was an original idea when he wrote it, had been copied by so many other writers, it was his duty to make his next book as different as it could possibly be. His unusual modesty, his refusal to discuss his " Lewis Carroll " books with anyone, and his decision to read no more reviews of any of his works, all prevented him from realising that he and he alone could write books in the *Alice* style—and that not one of the imitations would be remembered, or indeed was worthy to be spoken of in the same breath with any-thing of his. Even the best of all the imitations—which Dodgson himself read and gave to Maggie Bowman—has long been forgotten : this is called *Wanted—A King*, and was written by Margaret Hamer (only she used the name of " Maggie Browne ")—none of whose stories for children are read today.

Sylvie and Bruno makes one feel almost as if Dodgson had written a story in nearly the *Alice* style, then cut it up into unequal bits, and fitted these very ingeniously into an interesting, but not very good society novel—which was itself made up largely of stray ideas and scraps of sermons. Many of the stray ideas are excellent and often very amusing ; some scraps of sermon are beautiful, devout and true ; but it is the fairy-tale which counts, and had he concentrated on that, we might have had another real classic to put on the same shelf with *Alice*—even if it must always take just the second place.

People seem dimly to have realised this, for in 1904 Charles Dodgson's brother Edwin, while recovering from an illness, tried to pick out the fairy-tale, and issued the result separately as *The Story of Sylvie and Bruno*. He was only partly successful, for he was so careful not to add more than a few connecting words of his own, that the story still does not hang together properly—and as he dared not alter or re-write anything, many of the best scenes had to be left out, as they were partly concerned with the characters in the novel. In the original book it is hard enough to know where things are happening and who the people are—but in the *Story* it becomes quite impossible, and people we have never heard of begin to speak, though they were not even there a moment before. If Charles shows some signs of having forgotten what children really like, Edwin almost proves that he himself has never known !

But it is rather ungrateful to find fault with Edwin Dodgson's efforts, for many children who would have missed *Sylvie and Bruno* otherwise, have come to it by means of his version : and it is a story which should on no account be missed.

Charles Dodgson himself thought more highly of it than of any of his books—perhaps because it cost him so much trouble and hard work to write—and he took far more pains to get it properly illustrated than he had ever done with *Alice*.

The very first idea for the book was the little fairy-tale "Bruno's Revenge" which appeared in *Aunt Judy's Magazine* for December, 1867. Almost at once the editor, Mrs. Gatty, begged him to write some more stories about Sylvie and Bruno, and make a whole series of them, but he replied that he had no time and could not think of any ideas for them. However at the end of 1872, when he was staying at Hatfield House with the Marquis of Salisbury, he told some further adventures of the two fairy children to the young people there assembled (including at least one real Princess); and a couple of years later he was telling the dreadful fate of Uggug to the same children.

It was about this time that he thought of writing the book, and certainly he began to make notes for it, jotting down anything he happened to think of which might be of some use, and adding a number of amusing remarks made by children, such as that of the little boy who, when told not to pull the dog's tail, remarked: "But it doesn't bite at *that* end!"

Dodgson himself tells us how the story was put together: "And thus it came to pass that I found myself at last in possession of a huge unwieldy mass of litterature—if the reader will excuse the spelling—which only needed stringing together upon the thread of a consecutive story, to constitute the book I hoped to write. Only! the task at first seemed absolutely hopeless . . . and I think it must have been ten years or more before I had succeeded in classifying these odds-and-ends sufficiently to see what sort of a story they indicated : for the story had to grow out of the incidents, not the incidents out of the story."

But well before the end of those ten years Dodgson, besides collecting his material, was looking round for an illustrator, and when he found that Tenniel would not undertake the book for him, he decided to ask Walter Crane, whose illustrations of children he had seen and admired in Mrs. Molesworth's earlier stories, such as *Carrots* and *The*

Cuckoo Clock. He wrote to him at the end of 1877, and again early in the following year when he had already received an answer to say that Crane was interested and would like to hear more about the book : " As to terms, I quite see that it is fair to charge for two or three drawings at a higher rate than for a large number. But you did not at all misunderstand me : I am *not* contemplating a book with fifty pictures *now*. No such book is at present in existence. I was merely pointing out what it would come to if I *were* to write such a book and pay for the pictures at that rate. . . " (Dodgson, one must remember, always paid for the production of his books, including the whole cost of the illustrations and the cutting of the blocks from which they were printed). Crane accordingly declared himself willing to produce £60 worth of drawings within a year as specimens for the whole book; but, he writes, " my hands were so full of all sorts of other work that I fear the year went by without my being able to take the matter up. The story too, of which he sent me a portion, was of a very different character from Alice—a story with a religious and moral purpose, with only an occasional touch of the ingenuity and humour of *Alice*, so that it was not nearly so inspiring or amusing. . ."

Walter Crane did nothing about the illustrations, and Dodgson finally gave him up in despair. Next he approached Randolph Caldecott, but with no better success. Whether he then tried anyone else is uncertain ; he may have asked Henry Holiday (for one picture by him of Sylvie and Bruno is in existence), and decided that his type of drawing was not what he wanted ; but on March 1, 1885, he wrote to a very well-known caricaturist of the day, Harry Furniss, asking if he would be interested in the work. Furniss replied at once that he had long wished to illustrate a book by " Lewis Carroll," and was quite prepared to begin immediately on *Sylvie and Bruno*, and

Dodgson wrote back delightedly on March 10 : "I have a considerable mass of chaotic materials for a story, but have never had the heart to go to work to construct the story as a whole, owing to its seeming so hopeless that I should ever find a suitable artist. Now that you are found, I shall go back to my *Alice in Wonderland* style of work with every hope of making a success."

Harry Furniss, meeting Tenniel at about this time, told him that he was going to illustrate Dodgson's new book, and Tenniel exclaimed : "I'll give you a week, old chap ; *you* will never put up with that fellow a day longer." " You'll see," answered Furniss. " If I like the work, I shall manage the author ! " " Not a bit of it," insisted Tenniel, " Lewis Carroll is impossible ! You will see that my prophecy will come true ! " and he went on to declare that he himself could not tolerate " that conceited old don " any more.

Furniss was much impressed by Dodgson when he met him, and writes that he " was as unlike any other man as his books were unlike any other author's books. It was a relief to meet the pure, simple, innocent dreamer of children, after the selfish, commercial mind of most authors. Carroll was a wit, a gentleman, a bore and an egotist—and, like Hans Andersen, a spoilt child. . . Carroll was not selfish, but a liberal-minded, liberal-handed philanthropist, but his egotism was all but second childhood."

Harry Furniss has left on record a great deal about his dealings with Dodgson over *Sylvie and Bruno*, but one is inclined to feel that occasionally his imagination has been drawn on rather than his memory—and surely so great a caricaturist as Furniss must, quite without realising it, have come to remember in caricature just as he could not draw without it—as his sketches of Dodgson show !

However, mindful of Tenniel's warning, and having arrived at his own conclusions about his strange employer, Furniss settled himself (according to his own story) to

" solve Lewis Carroll." He began by pretending to be
" wilful and erratic, bordering on insanity. We therefore
got on splendidly . . . ! " If he was posing, he considered that
Dodgson was too—for the lengths to which his desire for
secrecy was driven were almost unbelievable. " He informed
my wife that she was the most privileged woman in the
world," writes Furniss, " for she knew the man who knew
his ideas—that ought to content her. . . Furthermore,
he sent me an elaborate document to sign committing myself
to secrecy. This I indignantly declined to sign. ' My word
is as good as my bond,' I said, and, striking an attitude,
I hinted that I would ' strike,' inasmuch as I would not
work for years isolated from my wife and friends. I was
therefore no doubt looked upon by him as a lunatic. That
was what I wanted. . . "

After this, Dodgson began by sending him one or two
of the poems to illustrate, and followed this by descriptions
of scenes in the story—but not by even a part of the book
itself, which was quite probably still in a state of notes.

In March 1886 Furniss had not been shown any of the
book which he was illustrating, but Dodgson did send him a
copy of *Bruno's Revenge* as it has originally appeared in *Aunt
Judy's Magazine*, remarking of Sir F. Gilbert's illustration
to it that the children " both look grown-up, and something
like a blacksmith and a ballet dancer. . . Another thing
should be remembered, the *narrator* (the whole book will
be autobiographical) must not appear in *any* of the illustrations." And, just to puzzle poor Furniss even more,
he went on : " I think I had better explain part of the plot
as to these two—they are not fairies right through the book
—but *children*, though not in the real English life of the
narrator, but in a sort of dreamland, of the events of which
he is conscious. In their own home they are royal, or at
least of high rank. They run away and become fairies for a
while—in which state the narrator meets them, and is even

enabled to take them into his real life, where his friends suppose them to be ordinary children (of course they grow for this purpose ; in the enclosed story they must be only a few inches high). All these conditions make their *dress* rather a puzzle. They mustn't have wings, that is clear. And it mustn't be *quite* the common dress of London life. It must be as fanciful as possible—so as *just* to be presentable in Society. . . "

Then there was a lot of correspondence about the costume, Dodgson at first suggesting naked fairies, as in the fairy-tales illustrated by Dicky Doyle and other artists earlier in the century, but finally deciding that it would shock " Mrs. Grundy "—as the personification of exaggerated propriety used always to be called. Dodgson was not one of the people who see offence where no offence is meant, and was always ready to challenge any pose or fashion which he considered to be foolish ; but he was always quite ready to see, and to respect other people's feelings—even if he did not share them himself : to most people Dodgson's sensitiveness to anything which seemed to him irreverent, must have appeared just as exaggerated. About fashions in dress Dodgson had also decided opinions : " Next to the unapproachable ugliness of ' crinoline,' " he wrote to Furniss, " I think that these high shouldered sleeves are the worst things invented for ladies in our time. Imagine how horrified they would be if one of their daughters were *really* shaped like that ! . . . One thing more. *Please* don't give Sylvie high heels. They are an abomination to me. . . "

The dislike of high-heeled or pointed-toed shoes he carried into real life ; and Isa ruefully remembers the healthy but hideous square-toed creations which he caused to be made specially for her !

Harry Furniss continued with the illustrations for some time according to Dodgson's instructions, but at last he demanded to see the whole book before he could continue. He himself says that Dodgson thereupon cut up the manuscript into pieces, pasted them on to pages in haphazard order, marked them with numbers, letters and hieroglyphics, and sent the whole to him in this condition—the idea being that no one should be able to read it who did not possess the key to the arrangement of the pieces. This sounds rather a tall story, but the probable explanation is that the book was still not properly put together, and what Dodgson sent was really the unwieldy mass of " litterature," classified but not yet written out in consecutive order !

However, Furniss got his own back a little later, when the illustrations seemed to be so far advanced that Dodgson suddenly turned up to see them. Now Furniss was a man who liked to work quickly and get a large amount done at one time, and *not* to turn out one drawing each month as Dodgson imagined he was doing : therefore there was not a single illustration to be seen ! But Furniss was equal to the occasion, and thus he tells the tale :

" Lewis Carroll came from Oxford one evening . . . to dine, and afterwards to see a batch of the work. He ate little, drank little, but enjoyed a few glasses of sherry, his favourite wine.

" Now," he said, " for the studio ! "

" I arose and led the way. My wife sat in astonishment. She knew I had nothing to show. Through the drawing-room, down the steps of the conservatory to the door of my studio. My hand is on the handle. Through excitement Lewis Carroll stammers worse than ever. Now to see the work for his great book ! I pause, turn my back to the closed door, and thus address the astonished don :

" ' Mr. Dodgson, I am *very* eccentric—I cannot help it ! Let me explain to you clearly before you enter my studio, that my eccentricity sometimes takes a violent form. If I, in showing my work, see the slightest sign that you are not *absolutely* satisfied with any particle of this work in progress, the *whole* of it goes into the fire! It is a risk: will you accept it, or will you wait till I have the drawings *quite* finished and send them to Oxford?'"

"'I-I-I ap-p-appreciate your feelings—I-I- should feel the same myself. I am off to Oxford!' and he went. . ."

A good story, even if perhaps a little bit exaggerated!

And so the long process of illustrations went on, the date of publication being put off from year to year, until finally Dodgson decided to issue the book in two parts (each as long as both *Alice* books put together!)—*Sylvie and Bruno* in 1889, and *Sylvie and Bruno Concluded* in 1893—though, of course, they are no more than volumes I and II of the same book.

The critics, who expected another *Alice*, were disappointed—and said so. This did not trouble Dodgson, however, for in the preface to the second volume he says that he has carefully avoided reading any reviews of the first, lest praise should make him conceited or blame prove too depressing. But of the difficulties which many readers found in following the sudden change of scene in the story, he did take note, and wrote a most interesting letter on the subject to the *St. James's Gazette* in January, 1890, headed *Sylvie and Bruno* : " You will, I believe, be doing a kindness to many readers of this book, who have found difficulties unforeseen by me, in the sudden change of scene, and the introduction into real life of what they suppose to be ' dream-children,' if you will allow me to explain that the book is written on the theory of the actual existence of fairies, and of their being able to assume human form. The ' I ' of the story goes through three different stages of being (1) real life, (2) the ' eerie ' stage in which he can see fairies, (3) trance, in which while his body remains apparently asleep, his spirit is free to pass into fairyland and witness what is going on there at the moment. There are no 'dreams' in the book: the many imitations that have appeared of my two 'dream-stories' have effectually barred me from any further attempt to write fiction of that kind."

One must not, of course, assume that Dodgson actually believed in fairies—and the " I " (or " Mister Sir," as Bruno calls him) of the story need not be he ; though he is actually called Lewis Carroll in the original " Bruno's Revenge "— but they are worked in and out of the story very convincingly.

The book itself (counting both volumes together, of course) could not possibly be retold here as a whole. The characters do very little—except talk, and this they do prodigiously, airing Dodgson's views, telling Dodgson's humorous stories and discussing Dodgson's ingenious puzzles : indeed, after the fairy-tale, the conversations are the best things in the book, and some of them are as amusing as anything in *Alice*.

But the best thing of all, of course, is the story of Sylvie and Bruno. Looking at their doings only, and trying to forget the numerous interruptions caused by the other parts of the book, we might reconstruct their adventures in some such continuous form as this :

They are the children of the Warden of Outland, a province of Fairyland, but far removed from Elfland, which is the real Fairy country. The Warden has to go to Elfland to compete for the Emperorship of Fairyland, and leaves his wicked brother and sister-in-law, Sibimet and Tabikat, to rule in Outland, advised by the Court Professor. These two conspire to make themselves King and Queen and to put their horrible son Uggug in Bruno's place as heir-presumptive. They ill-treat the two children so much that, with the help of the Professor and the Mad Gardener, they run away to look for their father, and find the way to

Elfland by means of Sylvie's magic locket. On the way they pass through Dogland and have an amusing time with the canine population. Once in Elfland, they become fairies, and live happily for a time, their daily life being described in such chapters as "Bruno's Revenge," "Bruno's Picnic," and so on. But at last the Professor arrives with the news that Sibimet and Tabikat are about to be crowned king and queen, and he returns with Sylvie and Bruno to delay the coronation until the Warden can appear with full powers as Emperor. When their "real life" adventures happen is hard to tell: perhaps on the way back to Outland; but certainly they visit Lady Muriel, in company with "Mister Sir" (who has followed their Outland adventures in the "trance" state and their Elfland adventures in the "eerie" state), mystifying her with a bunch of fairy flowers, with a "phlizz" (a magic likeness of a person that just disappears when shaken), and by their odd remarks.

When they return to Outland a great coronation banquet is about to begin, and before it starts the Professor gives the lecture which he has been preparing throughout the book. Half-way through the banquet things begin to happen: Uggug turns into a porcupine, and the Warden arrives just in time to prevent his brother's wicked plans from succeeding. And all ends happily with forgiveness and a beautiful sunset.

This is a very bald outline of the story, and does almost no justice to its real merits at all—for these, as in *Alice*, are to be found mainly in what people say, and in little incidents that are scarcely part of the main plot. The Professor is almost a second White Knight, and his inventions are just as amusing:

" But what's the use of wearing umbrellas round one's knees ? "

" In *ordinary* rain," the Professor admitted, " they would not be of much use. But if ever it rained horizontally, you know, they would be invaluable—simply invaluable!"

While his remarks are every bit as logical as those of the King of Hearts:

"The Professor put his hands over his ears, with a look of dismay. 'If you once let him begin a *Poem*,' he said to Sylvie, 'he'll never leave off again! He never does!' 'Did he ever begin a Poem and not leave off again.' Sylvie enquired. 'Three times,' said the Professor. . ."

And frequently he combines the two, as in his plan for preventing cold feet:

"That's the *shoemaker's* fault!" the Professor cheerfully replied. "How often I've explained to him that he *ought* to make boots with little iron frames under the soles to hold lamps! But he never *thinks*. No one would suffer from cold, if they would *think* of those little things. I always use hot ink, myself, in the winter. Very few people ever think of *that*. Yet how simple it is!"

Another delightful character is the Mad Gardener, whose logic is good (as when Bruno points out that he is watering the garden with an empty can, and he explains that he always does so because it's lighter to hold) and whose songs are better—nine songs (or nine verses of the same song) of which any example will do:

> "He thought he saw a Rattlesnake
> That questioned him in Greek:
> He looked again, and found it was
> The Middle of Next Week.
> 'The one thing I regret,' he said,
> 'Is that it cannot speak!' . . ."

But the book is full of such delights, and it would be a real tragedy should it be forgotten, even if it is not quite so spontaneous as *Alice* and certainly not so faultlessly constructed.

Dodgson had almost a morbid fear of there being any possible link between *Alice* and *Sylvie*: "Anything which would have the effect of connecting the book with *Alice* would be absolutely disastrous," he wrote to Furniss. " I am trying my very best to get out of the old groove and to have no ' connecting-link ' whatever. . . ." Yet one link there is—between the last line of the one and the first line of the other : the acrostic poem to Alice Liddell which ends *Through the Looking-Glass* has for its final line : " Life, what is it but a dream," and the first line of the acrostic poem which dedicates *Sylvie and Bruno* to Isa Bowman runs : " Is all our life then but a dream ? "

If life were to him but a dream, he was destined to the true awakening not very many years after *Sylvie and Bruno Concluded* had appeared in 1893. People who knew Dodgson comparatively well, such as Professor York Powell, have said that " he had very good health and was seldom out of sorts for a day " ; yet during the last ten or fifteen years of his life, this does not seem always to have been the case. A letter to Mrs. Daniel in 1883 runs : " I fear I must ask you not to come tomorrow. I am not quite ' the thing,' and in fact am fit for little else than to lie on the sofa all day and read novels," and the shaky writing of this letter suggests that he was rather seriously ill, though it was quite in accordance with his characters to disguise the fact as much as possible. Perhaps the collections of novels which he made may suggest that this was far from being a unique state, for he said frequently that he had no time for any reading, owing to the pressure of work ; novels, as the only diet possible when " not quite the thing " would be considered as beside the point. But as well as his numerous books on mathematics, logic and theology, his library consisted mainly of contemporary poetry, including most first editions of Tennyson, Keats, Rossetti and Browning, and the earlier volumes of Morris, Swinburne and Edwin Arnold—and novels, also usually in first editions, including nearly complete sets of Dickens, Scott, the Brontes, Miss Thackeray, Mrs. Craik, George Meredith, Fennimore Cooper, both Kingsleys, George MacDonald, Besant, Robert Louis Stevenson and Rudyard Kipling. He had also a fair number of children's books—perhaps intended firstly for his child-friends—including *The Rose and the Ring*, *The Water Babies*, and many by Mrs. Molesworth, Mrs. Ewing, George MacDonald and Jean Ingelow. At the time of his death his two favorite authors seem to have been Rudyard Kipling and J. M. Barrie—so he was at least always up to date!

Whether or not he kept all these for times of illness, his health was becoming less settled by the early 'Nineties, and in 1891 he was writing to Harry Furniss that he was " rather seriously ill . . . I don't think I have any right to reckon much on the coming years, and there is a lot of work I want to finish before the end comes." And frequently while he was preparing *Sylvie and Bruno* he was writing to various people of his anxiety to get the book finished as soon as possible in case anything should happen to him.

Probably he worked too hard, and over-taxed his brain and his nervous energy : certainly he suffered more and more acutely from what his nephew describes as " seeing fortifications moving across his eyes "—which is almost certainly that inexplicable malady known as " Doctor's Migraine," where the hindered vision is followed after an hour or so by a couple of hours of almost unbearable headache, and often as much as two days of pains in the head which suggest to the unfortunate sufferer that the nerves of or in his brain have become like piano wires screwed half a turn too tight—a sensation which makes any serious brain work almost impossible.

One will never know how often Dodgson suffered from these attacks, nor whether they grew more frequent towards the end of his life—for he made light of any hardships of his own, and continued working during most hours of the day and many of the night, and devoting all his powers of understanding and amusing to the child-friends whom he continued to make, and the friends among older girls and young women whose acquaintance he began to cultivate more and more after about 1890.

In writing he spent most of his time preparing *Symbolic Logic*, only the first of the three parts of which was ever published (in 1896). Another scheme, on which he was working at the end of 1897, was his book of *Original Games and Puzzles*, but he kept allowing himself to be led off into disputes over obscure points in logic or mathematics, and this book also never appeared.

At the end of November he spent a day in London to see Barrie's play *The Little Minister*, " a beautiful play, beautifully acted," he calls it, and says that he should like to see it " again and again."

Just before Christmas Dodgson went as usual to stay with his sisters at their house " The Chestnuts " in Guildford, where he was working hard every day on the second part of *Symbolic Logic*. But on January 6, 1898, a slight attack of influenza prevented him from reading family prayers, as he was accustomed to do every morning at Guildford, and later in the day he retired to bed. At first he did not seem to be seriously ill, but in less than a week bronchial symptoms developed and his breathing became hard and laborious. By the 13th he knew that the end was at hand : " take away those pillows," he said, " I shall need them no more," and he lay back, still breathing heavily. And on the 14th, at half-past two in the afternoon the heavy breathing ceased quietly, and he fell asleep.

He was buried in the lonely cemetery up on the downs in Guildford :

" A marble cross, under the shadow of a pine, marks the spot," writes his nephew and biographer Stuart Dodgson

Collingwood, "and beneath his own name they have engraved the name of 'Lewis Carroll,' that the children who pass by may remember their friend, who is now . . . in that 'Wonderland' which outstrips all our dreams."

CHAPTER X

LEWIS CARROLL

AND now the time has come " to talk of many things," and to see if we can understand a little of how it came about that the Rev. Charles Lutwidge Dodgson of Christ Church, Oxford, was able to write books which come nearer to the heart of childhood and to the child which is in almost every heart, than those of any other great writer —books that have made the pen-name " Lewis Carroll " famous throughout the world and beloved of many million readers, old as well as young.

Charles Dodgson understood children; he had every opportunity for observing them, and he was by profession a trained observer and relater of minute details. But he had a far greater gift besides, and a far rarer one : not only could he study children from outside, he could enter into their thoughts, look at life through their eyes, ponder over it with their minds, and then interpret what he thus saw and felt with the full understanding of a cultured adult intellect.

But his relations with grown-up people were always rather cold and distant ; in their company he felt nervous, and as he could not speak to them without stammering, that made the nervousness worse.

Yet, of course, he was very natural, " as firm and self-contained as a man may be," as Isa bears testimony. " You could easily discern it in the way in which he met and talked with his friends. When he shook hands with you— he had firm white hands, rather large—his grip was strong and steadfast. . . Everyone says when he shook your hand the pressure of his was full of strength, and you felt here indeed was a man to admire and to love."

Dodgson was a good-looking man, of medium height, with clear-cut, delicate and rather sensitive features, and a very upright carriage, though he walked a trifle jerkily.

It seems odd that no one fell in love with him when he was a young man; but then his shyness and his feeling of being "out of it" must have made him awkward and distant whenever young ladies were present. And he himself almost certainly fell in love with somebody, probably round about the year 1860, or just a little earlier: his nephew, who wrote the only satisfactory biography that has yet appeared, suggests that this was so, but very rightly gives no details—and details do not matter. But there was a shadow of sadness over his life, a shadow which, far from souring him, made him even more able to sympathise with others who were in trouble and to understand and comfort their sorrows.

This one early sadness was Dodgson's only love affair— though to be sure clever people have suggested (without a shred of evidence) that he was in love with Alice Liddell and with Ellen Terry!—and he lost the one supreme chance of escaping from the vicious circle of shyness, stammering and sense of being cut off, and was left with only his growing hosts of child-friends who had already become one of the main concerns of his life by the time Alice Liddell was too old to be amused by tales told on river picnics.

In consequence, his understanding of children increased, and with it his ability to think and imagine as they did, of living in Wonderland for long enough at a time to learn its really authentic language and bring a sufficient number of " dream-rushes," " plucked in a far off land," to weave his two stories of *Alice*.

But by the end of *Through the Looking-Glass* he was asking " Life, what is it but a dream ? " and when *Sylvie and Bruno* was ready, the feeling was almost a statement of accepted fact, " Is all our life, then, but a dream ? "

This affected his work to some extent: even as early as 1876 when the *Snark* appeared, Andrew Lang, reviewing it for *The Academy*, put his finger on the trouble, complaining that excellent though the nonsense was, it had no *living* character such as Alice, and so was just too far from reality to have quite as perfect an effect as the earlier books. And of course *Sylvie and Bruno* proves this suggestion to the hilt: Dodgson is quite out of touch with real life when he (and " Mister Sir ") try to understand the lives lived by Lady Muriel and the Earl, Eric Lindon and Arthur Forrester— they are scarcely possible, far less are they probable! But the fairy children are real still, and so is the Professor (who is only a child with a bald head), and Dodgson can understand them and reproduce all that he sees and knows of them, thanks to his still developing gift of re-entering childhood. But even here the growingly artificial outlook on grown-up life intruded occasionally; Sylvie in contact with humans is a little too good to be true, her sweetness just once in a while self-conscious.

Had Dodgson married in, say, 1860, and thus come closer to the truth and fullness of life, instead of seeing it more and more through a closed window, *Sylvie and Bruno* might easily have been as much greater than *Alice* as *Alice* is than the stories in the family magazines of his Croft days.

On the purely literary side, too, he would have been saved from his obsessions about originality and about showing his unpublished work to nobody whatsoever. When he wrote *Sylvie and Bruno* he proved that the power of criticising his own work from the point of view of the suitability and unity of the parts in a single work of art had completely deserted him. Yet he was intensely pleased with *Sylvie and Bruno*, serenely assured that *this* was his best and greatest work!

But we must not spend too long on considering what Dodgson might have done; what he did is already included among the great literature of the world. Yet it is emphatically the man and what he is that makes the books what they are—and Charles Dodgson and no other was the author of *Alice*.

Almost from the moment of his death people have been obsessed by the strange idea that the author of Alice was a " dual personality," and that Lewis Carroll was most unlike Charles Dodgson and did not get on at all well with him. They have even gone so far as to say that Dodgson (or Carroll ?) himself (themselves ?) realised this and made self-conscious jokes about it (that is, the Lewis Carroll self was conscious, and made jokes about the unfortunate Mr. Dodgson, who wasn't). Now the only reason for keeping up the distinction of Lewis Carroll the author from C. L. Dodgson the don, was that he hated publicity, and to be " lionised," and wished to remain personally unknown. A letter in the *St. James's Gazette* in 1890 disclosed Lewis Carroll's real name, and Dodgson wrote privately to the new editor, Sidney Low, begging him to decline in future to print " any statement as to my connection with the ' nom de plume ' of ' Lewis Carroll ' . . . it being my earnest wish to remain, personally, in the obscurity of a private individual. In fact, it is for that very purpose that I continue to use that ' nom de plume ' . . . "

But there is no indication that there was any more conflict in the mind of Charles Dodgson than in the mind of any other deeply serious and sensitive person. There was a shadow over one side of his life, but he was not soured by it, nor was he unhappy or a disappointed man in any other way. There was no disguise about him either : he was truly fond of his many child-friends, truly concerned in understanding them and making them happy, just as he was completely sincere in his religious views and a simple, straightforward Christian in all his ways. One has only to read his two or three published sermons (one of them meant specially for children) to appreciate the constant reality of his religion; and those who heard him preach bear witness to the intensity and realism of the conviction behind everything he said.

Of course, his lonely life and the lack of a mature companion with whom no subject was barred, tended to make him over apt to worry away at little doubts as to ethics or religion, and magnify them far beyond their proper importance. In the same way his lonely life and his constant work as a mathematician and a logician tended to make him more and more precise and orderly, and to foster the odd little tricks of the man living alone into the complicated system of gadgets, registers and regulations with which he came to surround himself.

The long, long hours spent in the study of exact and prosaic sciences almost of themselves demanded nonsense as a reaction; the constant companionship of small children made the form of nonsense inevitable; and the fascination with the meanings of words common to the writer and the logician produced the kind of nonsense.

But it was Charles Dodgson in whom was fulfilled all these conditions, and who as a result produced the books associated with the name of Lewis Carroll. And to his child-friends there was only " Uncle Dodgson "; after a first meeting he might sign himself Lewis Carroll, just because they still knew *Alice* better than they knew him; but very soon they were coming to visit Uncle Dodgson, to listen to his stories, solve his puzzles and talk to him as to the most wonderful of equals.

Grown people who met Dodgson on formal occasions have said again and again how dull he was, how impossible it was to believe that this silent, rather boring don was the author of *Alice*. There was Mark Twain, for example, who records that during a visit to England he met " a great many interesting people, among them Lewis Carroll, author of the immortal *Alice*—but he was only interesting to look at, for he was the stillest and shyest full grown man I have ever met, except ' Uncle Remus '. . . Several other lively talkers were present, and the talk went briskly on for a couple of hours, but Carroll sat still all the while except that now and then he answered a question. His answers were brief. I do not remember that he elaborated any of them."

Such recollections as these by people who hardly knew Dodgson at all do give support to the theory that Lewis Carroll was almost another person : but we have only to turn to what Professor York Powell, who did know him well and who was able to observe him in the Christ Church Common Room during many years, tells us, to meet the man as he really was, Charles Dodgson the one and only Lewis Carroll :

" The quiet humour of his voice, a very pleasant voice, the occasional laugh—he was not a man who often laughed, though there was often a smile playing about his sensitive mouth—and the slight hesitation that whetted some of his wittiest sayings—all those that knew him must remember ; but his kindly sympathies, his rigid rule of his own life, his dutiful discharge of every obligation that was in the slightest degree incumbent on him, his patience with his younger colleagues, who were sometimes a little ignorant and impatient of the conditions under which alone Common Room life must be in the long-run ruled, his rare modesty, and the natural kindness which preserved him from the faintest shadow of conceit, and made him singularly courteous to everyone, high or low, he came across in his quiet academic life—these his less known characteristics will only remain in the memories of his colleagues and contemporaries. Dodgson and Liddon long made the House Common Room a resort where the weary brain-worker found harmless mirth and keen but kindly wit. . . Dodgson was a good teller of anecdote, a fantastic weaver of parodox and propounder of puzzle, a person who never let the talk flag, but never monopolised it, who had rather set others talking than talk himself, and was as pleased to hear a twice-told tale as to retail his own store of reminiscences. . . "

Hardly any of Dodgson's Common Room stories have been preserved : one chance visitor in 1870 heard him tell the tale of the man whose feet were so large that he had to put on his trousers over his head ; and when dining out he told of the dog who was fetching out the sticks thrown for him into the sea : " He brought them back very properly for some time, and then there appeared to be a little difficulty, and he returned swimming in a very curious manner. On closer inspection it appeared that he had caught hold of his own tail by mistake, and was bringing it to land in triumph."

Or again, in a lecture called *Feeding the Mind* which he delivered in October, 1884, to a grown-up audience in Derbyshire, he says, by way of illustration : " It would fare but ill with many of us if we were left to superintend our own digestion and circulation. ' Bless me ! ' one would cry, ' I forgot to wind up my heart this morning ! To think that it has been standing still for the last three hours ! ' ' I can't walk with you this afternoon ' a friend would say, ' as I have no less than eleven dinners to digest. I had to let them stand over from last week, being so busy, and my doctor says he will not answer for the consequence if I wait any longer ! ' . . . "

Such examples as these show clearly how very much a part of himself was the vein of logical nonsense whence *Alice* was hewn. And more, far more is this shown by the letters (nearly two hundred have been published so far) which he wrote to his child-friends. These often have grave passages : does a child need to be given a new prayer and a new riddle, Dodgson will supply them both with perfect harmony, realising, as George MacDonald realised, that it is only " the heart that is not yet sure of its God that is afraid to laugh in His presence." But usually the letters are sheer light-hearted nonsense—nonsensical with the delicious prosaicness which shows the true understanding of the child's reactions, as in the following letter written to Magdalen Millard in 1875 (yet critics who have forgotten what it was to be a child have solemnly quoted this very letter in an attempt to show how uncomfortable Lewis Carroll always felt whenever he remembered that there was such a person in the world as C. L. Dodgson) :

" My dear Magdalen,

I want to explain to you why I did not call yesterday. I was sorry to miss you, but you see I had so many conversations on the way. I tried to explain to the people in the street that I was going to see you, but they wouldn't listen ; they said they were in a hurry, which was rude. At last I met a wheel-barrow that I thought would attend to me, but I couldn't make out what was in it. I saw some features at first, then I looked through a telescope and found it was a countenance ; then I looked through a microscope and found it was a face ! I thought it was rather like me, so I fetched a large looking-glass to make sure, and then to my great joy I found it was me. We shook hands, and were just beginning to talk, when myself came up and joined us, and we had quite a pleasant conversation. I said, ' Do you remember when we all met at Sandown ? ' and myself said, ' It was very jolly there ; there was a child called Magdalen,' and me said, ' I used to like her a little ; not much, you know—only a little.' Then it was time for us to go to the train, and who do you think came to the station to see us off ? You would never guess, so I must tell you. They were two very dear friends of mine, who happen to be here just now, and beg to be allowed to sign this letter as your affectionate friends,

LEWIS CARROLL and C. L. DODGSON."

Or again, there is the letter to Florence Terry explaining the lines from *Twelfth Night*. "She sat like patience on a monument, Smiling at grief." "This quotation," writes Dodgson with a fine show of seriousness, "is altogether a misprint. Let me explain it to you. The passage originally stood, '*They* sit like patients on the Monument, smiling at Greenwich.' In the next edition 'Greenwich' was printed short 'Greenh.,' and so got gradually altered into 'grief.' The allusion of course is to the celebrated Dr. Jenner, who used to send all his patients to sit on top of the Monument (near London Bridge) to inhale fresh air, promising them that, when they were well enough, they should go to 'Greenwich Fair.' So, of course, they always looked out towards Greenwich and sat smiling to think of the treat in store for them. . . The custom of sitting on the Monument was given up when Dr. Jenner went mad, and insisted on it that the air was worse up there and that the *lower* you went the *more airy* it became. Hence he always called those little yards, below the pavement, outside the kitchen windows, '*the kitchen airies* !' a name that is still in use.

"All this information you are most welcome to use, the next time you are in want of something to talk about. You may say you learned it from 'a distinguished etymologist' which is perfectly true, since anyone who knows me by sight can easily distinguish me from all other etymologists. . ."

It was "nonsense" of this type, of the letter about sending things by the "post," and of a hundred other letters, that produced the supreme "nonsense" of *Alice*. It is a wild, fantastic imagination, a fancy as free and unfettered as a leaf in the wind, yet just as orderly as Dodgson's own life, worked out with the remorseless logic of a problem in mathematics, and presented in words whose every meaning is remembered, yet in a style as simple and direct as that of a theorem in Euclid. The bonds of everyday life are broken, but none of the rules are touched ; the stories are dreams only in the swift changes of scene, size and situation: otherwise, the characters are rather more awake than in real life. Much of it " came " to Dodgson, but not in a meaningless chaos as a dream comes, the jumbled echoes of the day's delights as at the end of each chapter in *Isa's Visit to Oxford*. *Alice in Wonderland* was constructed with care out of the more careless story actually told to the Liddells on their picnic ; *Through the Looking-Glass* was written with greater care still, and is much more of a perfect unity—yet its ground work was a series of casual inventions about chessmen coming to life, told some years before the book was written and remembered with sufficient dimness to melt and mold together into the new story; perhaps the only concrete things before Dodgson when he began to write were the poems " Jabberwocky " and " Upon the Lonely Moor " : the White Knight was certainly invented simply as the sort of person to recite that particular poem, and quite possibly Humpty-Dumpty became what he is for the express purpose of explaining the words in " Jabberwocky "—as now the footnotes of the *Misch-Masch* days would no longer do. But, most of all, the stories must have grown as they were written, and the inspiration must have been very largely that odd and unexpected thing the English Language :

" Alice . . . went on : ' Would you tell me please, which way I ought to go from here ? '

' That depends a good deal on where you want to get to,' said the Cat.

' I don't much care where—' said Alice.

' Then it doesn't matter which way you go,' said the Cat.

' So long as I get *somewhere*,' Alice added as an explanation.

' Oh, you are sure to do that,' said the Cat, ' if you only walk long enough.'

Alice felt that this could not be denied . . . "

Or again :

" ' I must have *two*, you know—to come and go. One to come and one to go.'

' I beg your pardon ? ' said Alice.

' It isn't respectable to beg,' said the King.

' I only meant that I didn't understand,' said Alice. ' Why one to come and one to go ? '

' Don't I tell you ? ' the King repeated impatiently. ' I must have *two*, to fetch and carry. One to fetch, and one to carry '." . . .

Or even the Professor's :

" ' Does you *always* confuses two animals together ? ' Bruno asked.

' Pretty often, I'm afraid,' the Professor candidly confessed. ' Now, for instance, there's the rabbit hutch and the hall-clock.' The Professor pointed them out. ' One gets a little confused with *them*—both having doors, you know. Now, only yesterday—would you believe it ?—I put some lettuces into the clock, and tried to wind up the rabbit ! '

' Did the rabbit *go*, after you wound it up ? ' said Bruno. The Professor clasped his hands on the top of his head, and groaned.

' Go ? I should think it *did* go. Why it's *gone* ! . . . ' "

And just in the same way Uncle Dodgson would write to Isa, gravely taking whatever she had said at its exact and literal value—just to see where it would lead them : " It's all very well for you and Nellie and Empsie to write in millions of hugs and kisses, but please consider the *time* it would occupy your poor old very busy Uncle ! Try hugging and kissing Empsie for a minute by the watch, and I don't think you'll manage it more than twenty times a minute. ' Millions ' must mean two millions at least. . . I couldn't go on hugging and kissing more than twelve hours a day : and I wouldn't like to spend *Sundays* that way. So you see it would take twenty three *weeks* of hard work. Really, my dear child, *I cannot spare the time ! . . .*"

But above all *Alice* was written with the aid of that wonderful power which Dodgson had of looking at anything he chose from the true angle of a real child—and of translating the child's reactions into vivid and reasoned language, curbed and directed by the brilliant mind of the grown man.

Further than this we cannot explain *Alice* any more than by saying that it is the work of a unique genius, a perfect blend of the child's simplicity with the mind of a mathematician who was also a very great writer. People who try to explain the books away as a sort of allegory of all the struggles and repressions in Dodgson's subconscious mind, merely show the nature of their own not very pleasant imaginations, and leave untouched the pure and simple soul of the true Lewis Carroll whom I have tried to picture for you in this book.

"Those who knew him and mourn his loss," wrote Bishop Strong, another Christ Church friend who knew Dodgson well, "are able to read between the lines of his books, and see there the working of the mind they knew; for, as we have said, the cast of his thought was very much the same in everything that he approached; the humour of *Alice* and the other books was one manifestation of an original and perhaps somewhat eccentric genius. And those who know him only through his books have a real knowledge of him; they are not looking at a mere fanciful product of his leisure, though they learn from others how natural it seemed that a clever, simple-hearted and religious man should express himself in books for children of all ages. . ."

THREE PANELS FROM THE LEWIS CARROLL MEMORIAL
WINDOW IN DARESBURY CHURCH, CHESHIRE

APPENDIX

WRITINGS BY AND ABOUT LEWIS CARROLL

The following is a list of Dodgson's more important and interesting works, most of which are mentioned in this book. Many of them will be known to all readers, and easily available, but some are very rare, and I have tried to indicate the easiest way of finding them.

In 1937 The Nonsuch Press published a glaring red volume called *The Complete Works of Lewis Carroll*, with an introduction by Alexander Woollcott. The book itself is far from being "complete" in any sense of the word, but it is none the less a most useful volume, containing things that would otherwise be hard, and in a few cases impossible, for the ordinary reader to find. Any item in the following list which is preceded by an asterisk is included in the Nonsuch volume.

A. BOOKS IN PROSE AND VERSE

*Alice's Adventures in Wonderland	1865
Bruno's Revenge—(In *Aunt Judy's Magazine*)	Dec. 1867
*Phantasmagoria, and Other Poems	1869
*Through the Looking-Glass, and What Alice Found There	1872
*Notes by an Oxford Chiel—[Six Oxford Pamphlets]...	1874
*The Hunting of the Snark	1876
*Rhyme ? and Reason ?	1883
*A Tangled Tale	1885
Alice's Adventures Underground	1886
The Nursery Alice	1889
*Sylvie and Bruno...	1889
*Eight or Nine Wise Words about Letter-Writing ...	1890
*Sylvie and Bruno Concluded	1893
*Three Sunsets, and Other Poems	1898
The Story of Sylvie and Bruno	1904
Feeding the Mind	1907
Tour [to Russia] in 1867...	1928

The Rectory Umbrella and Misch-Masch [family
     Magazines]   1932
*Collected Verse of Lewis Carroll   1932
 Selections from Letters to his Child-Friends   1933

B. ORIGINAL GAMES AND PUZZLES, ETC.

*Rules for Court Circular   1860
*Croquet Castles   1862
*The Alphabet Cipher   1868
*Puzzles from Wonderland (*Aunt Judy's Magazine*)   Dec. 1870
*Doublets—A Word Puzzle   1879
 Lanrick (1880)   1881
*Misch Masch : A Word Game   1882
*A Tangled Tale   1885
 The Game of Logic   1886
 Memoria Technica   1888
 Circular Billiards   1890
 The Wonderland Postage-Stamp Case...   1890
*A Postal Problem   1891
*Syzygies : A Word-Puzzle   1891
 A Logical Paradox   1894
*What Achilles said to the Tortoise (Logical Problem)   1894

C. SOME INTERESTING ESSAYS AND SHORT
PIECES

Alice on the Stage (Essay in *The Theatre*)   ...   April 1887
Children in Theatres (Letter in *St. James's Gazette*)
                                                July 19, 1887
The Stage and the Spirit of Reverence (*The Theatre*)   July 1888
Children's Sermon at St. Leonards   1897
Isa's Visit to Oxford (in Isa Bowman's *Lewis Carroll*)...   1899
A Visit to Tennyson (Letter in *The Strand Magazine*)   May 1901

     Of the items in Section C. all except " Children in Theatres "
and " A Visit to Tennyson " are to be found in *The Lewis
Carroll Picture Book* edited by Dodgson's nephew S. D.
Collingwood in 1899, together with other interesting selections
that cannot be found elsewhere such as "Lanrick" and "A
Logical Paradox " from section B. This also includes the six
Oxford Pamphlets (*Notes by an Oxford Chiel*) and a number of
puzzles and problems.

Of books about Charles Dodgson and his works there are a number; the first and best being *The Life and Letters of Lewis Carroll* by Stuart Dodgson Collingwood (1898): this is a long and intimate account of Dodgson's life, with many extracts from his Diary (which no other biographer has since been allowed to see), letters and personal memoirs. In 1899 Isa Bowman produced a little book of reminiscences *The Story of Lewis Carroll* dealing only with her own recollections of Dodgson, but giving the most attractive and vivid portrait of him during the last ten years of his life that we possess. Another child-friend, Beatrice Hatch, had already published some short notes in *The Strand Magazine* of April 1898; and Ethel M. Arnold followed suit in *The Windsor Magazine* of December 1929. In 1930 Mr. Walter De la Mare wrote the best of the critical essays on Dodgson's works, and it has since been published as a small book.

Perhaps the most fascinating book of all (after Collingwood's biography) is *A Handbook of the Literature of the Rev. C. L. Dodgson* produced in 1931 by S. H. Williams and Falconer Madan; it is a bibliography of everything by or about Dodgson up to that date, but each item is carefully described, and there are quotations, reprints of rare items, essays on *Alice* and everything one could wish for.

In 1932 an Exhibition was held in London to celebrate the Centenary of Dodgson's birth, and Madan prepared an interesting catalogue, again reprinting items not to be found elsewhere. In the same year *The Life of Lewis Carroll* by Langford Reed appeared; a pleasant book in its way, rather inaccurate, rather inclined to develop " theories " (Mr. Reed is a great believer in the " dual personality " of Dodgson and Carroll) but adding a few new reminiscences. And even more important was an essay in *The Cornhill Magazine* (July 1932) called " Alice's Recollections of Carrollian Days " narrated by Alice Liddell herself.

My own book makes few claims, except those of being an attempt to accept Dodgson as he was ; of trying to understand him in relation to his environment ; and of telling a plain story as interestingly as possible. New material has been placed at my disposal by the kind offices of the following : Miss Isa Bowman, Miss Nellie Bowman, Miss Empsie Bowman ; Mr. John Greenidge (son of Dodgson's child-friend Edith Lucy) ; the Rev. Professor Clement Rogers (Dodgson's god-son) ; Mr. F. J. H. Sanders ; Mr. George Speaight ; and the Librarian of Christ Church. Besides all the books mentioned above, I have consulted a large number of printed sources—magazine articles and memoirs of the period—too numerous to mention here.

ROGER LANCELYN GREEN

ILLUSTRATIONS ACKNOWLEDGMENTS

The following are reproduced by courtesy of Miss F. Menella Dodgson, the executor of Lewis Carroll :—

The photographs of Charles Dodgson* (*page* 141) (taken by W. Shawcross, Guildford), Alice Liddell (*page* 49), the three Liddell sisters* (*page* 59), the Rossetti family (*page* 99), and Dodgson's study at Christ Church, Oxford (*page* 133) (taken by Hills & Saunders, Oxford).

Those marked * above, as well as the line illustrations on *pages* 3, 7, 19, 22, 84, 91, 108-9 and 125, from *The Life and Letters of Lewis Carroll* by Stuart Dodgson Collingwood (published by T. Fisher Unwin, 1898).

The line illustrations on *pages* 5, 32, 51, 72-3 and 87, from *The Lewis Carroll Picture Book*, edited by Stuart Dodgson Collingwood (published by T. Fisher Unwin, 1899).

The (*frontispiece*) portrait of Lewis Carroll by Sir Hubert Herkomer, and the Dining Hall, at Christ Church, Oxford (*page* 25), are from photographs by Walter Scott, Bradford.

The photograph of Mary Badcock (*page* 69), is reproduced by courtesy of Mrs. G. H. P. Burne, the executor of Mr. Sidney Badcock.

The photograph of Ellen Terry (*page* 120) is reproduced by courtesy of Mr. Helmut Gernsheim, F.R.P.S.

The photograph of the panels from the Memorial Window in Daresbury Church, Cheshire (*page* 173), is reproduced by courtesy of the Rector, The Rev. W. L. M. Protheroe.

STORY BIOGRAPHIES

MR. ORAM'S STORY (Capt. Jas. Cook, R.N.)
by Aubrey de Selincourt

FORTUNE MY FOE (Sir Walter Raleigh)
by Geoffrey Trease

THE STORY OF LEWIS CARROLL
by Roger Lancelyn Green

THE STORY OF HANS ANDERSEN
by Esther Meynell

Dat